Easy Ch Cookbook

150 Chicken Recipes

By
Chef Maggie Chow
Copyright © 2015 by Saxonberg
Associates
All rights reserved

Published by
BookSumo, a division of Saxonberg
Associates
http://www.booksumo.com/

STAY TO THE END OF THE COOKBOOK AND RECEIVE....

I really appreciate when people, take the time to read all of my recipes.

So, as a gift for reading this entire cookbook you will receive a **massive collection of special recipes.**

Read to the end of and get my *Easy Specialty Cookbook Box Set for FREE*!

This box set includes the following:

1. *Easy Sushi Cookbook*

2. ***Easy Dump Dinner Cookbook***
3. ***Easy Beans Cookbook***

Remember this box set is about **EASY** cooking.

In the ***Easy Sushi Cookbook*** you will learn the easiest methods to prepare almost every type of Japanese Sushi i.e. *California Rolls, the Perfect Sushi Rice, Crab Rolls, Osaka Style Sushi*, and so many others.

Then we go on to *Dump Dinners*. Nothing can be easier than a Dump Dinner. In the ***Easy Dump Dinner Cookbook*** we will learn how to master our slow cookers and make some amazingly unique dinners that will take almost ***no effort***.

Finally in the ***Easy Beans Cookbook*** we tackle one of my favorite side dishes: Beans. There are so many delicious ways to make Baked Beans and Bean Salads that I had to share them.

So stay till the end and then keep on cooking with my *Easy Specialty Cookbook Box Set*!

About the Author.

Maggie Chow is the author and creator of your favorite *Easy Cookbooks* and *The Effortless Chef Series*. Maggie is a lover of all things related to food. Maggie loves nothing more than finding new recipes, trying them out, and then making them her own, by adding or removing ingredients, tweaking cooking times, and anything to make the recipe not only taste better, but be easier to cook!

For a complete listing of all my books please see my author page.

INTRODUCTION

Welcome to *The Effortless Chef Series*! Thank you for taking the time to download the *Easy Chicken Cookbook*. Come take a journey with me into the delights of easy cooking. The point of this cookbook and all my cookbooks is to exemplify the effortless nature of cooking simply.

In this book we focus on Chicken. You will find that even though the recipes are simple, the taste of the dishes is quite amazing.

So will you join me in an adventure of simple cooking? If the answer is yes (and I hope it is) please consult the table of contents to find the dishes you are most interested in. Once you are ready jump right in and start cooking.

— Chef Maggie Chow

TABLE OF CONTENTS

STAY TO THE END OF THE COOKBOOK AND RECEIVE..2

About the Author.................................. 5

Introduction 7

Table of Contents 8

Any Issues? Contact Me 25

Legal Notes... 26

Common Abbreviations...................... 27

Chapter 1: Easy Chicken Recipes........ 28

   Tagine 28

   (Moroccan Style I) 28

   Couscous VIII 32

   (Chicken, Cucumbers, and Parsley) 32

   Couscous IX 35

   (Lime and Chicken).......................... 35

   Couscous XIX................................... 38

(Cloves, Onions, Tomatoes, and Chicken) 38

(Moroccan Style IV) 38

Couscous XXI 42

(Spicy Chicken and Carrots) 42

Couscous XXXIII 45

(Cucumbers, Capers, and Dates) 45

Couscous XXXV 48

(Carrots, Harissa, Peppers, Chicken, and Sausage) 48

Couscous XXXIX 52

(Tomatoes and Tarragon) 52

CHICKEN ADOBO 55

Chicken Mascarpone Pesto 58

Feta, Chicken, and Rosemary 62

(Greek Style Kebabs) 62

MEDITERRANEAN PASTA 65

CHICKEN SOUVLAKI 68

EASY GREEK STYLE CHICKEN BREASTS 72

CHICKEN SOUP 75

EASIEST GREEK CHICKEN 78

Chicken Souvlaki II 81
Indonesian Classical Satay 84
Satay Ayam 87
(Indo chicken with Peanut Sauce) 87
Chicken & Broccoli 91
Chicken Wings in Japan 94
(鶏手羽肉) 94
Fried Chicken 97
(フライドチキン) 97
Katsu 100
Tak Toritang 102
(Potato and Chicken) 102
Korean Teriyaki 105
Bulgogi II 108
(Korean Chicken Stir Fry) 108
Chicken from Korea 111
Korean Chicken Stew 114
Chili II 117
(Chicken, Peppers, and Jalapenos) 117
Chili V 120

(Rustic) 120
Chili X 123
(White Beans) 123
Chili XII 126
(White Beans and Tomatillos) 126
Asparagus XI 129
(Red Peppers, Mozzarella, and Chicken) 129
Asparagus V 132
(Tarragon, Lemons, and Provolone) 132
Asparagus VI 135
(Parmesan and Penne) 135
Asparagus XVI 138
(Chicken Stuffed) 138
Asparagus XXIV 141
(Asian Stir Fry) 141
Asparagus XXVI 144
(Thai Style) 144
Dumplings 147

Lemony Stuffed Chicken with Bacon 150

Baked Chicken Done Right 153

Buffalo Bacon Sandwich 156

Maggie's Easy Fried Rice............... 159

Chicken Breast I........................... 162

(Restaurant Style) 162

Chicken Breast II 165

(Lemon Pepper and Monterey) 165

Chicken Breast III 168

(Stuffed I) 168

(Sun Dried Tomatoes, Feta, and Spinach).. 168

Chicken Breast IV 172

(Pineapple, Brown Sugar, and Onions) 172

Chicken Breast V........................... 176

(Easy Italian Seasoned).................. 176

Chicken Breast VI 179

(Stuffed II) 179

(Bacon, Garlic, and Feta) 179

Chicken Breast VII 182
(Lemon, Dijon, and Rosemary) 182
Chicken Breast VIII 185
(Easy Flame Broiled) 185
Chicken Breast IX 188
(Easy Italian Style) 188
Chicken Breast X 192
(Stuffed III) 192
(Easy Creole Style) 192
Chicken Breast XI 196
(Cream of Chicken, Stuffing, and Swiss) 196
Chicken Breast XII 199
(Onions, Bacon, and Brown Sugar) 199
Chicken Breast XIII 203
(Lemon Lime Soda) 203
Chicken Breast XIV 206
(Easy Japanese Style) 206
Chicken Breast XV 209
(Tomatoes and Onions) 209
Chicken Breast XVI 212

(Rustic Style) 212

Chicken Breast XVII 215

(Savory Garlic) 215

Chicken Breast XVIII 218

(Teriyaki, Tomatillos, and Muenster) 218

Chicken Breast XIX 222

(Dump Dinner Style) 222

Chicken Breast XX 225

(Mozzarella, Rosemary, and Marsala) 225

Chicken Breast XXI 228

(Buttery Mushrooms and Cheese) . 228

Chicken Breast XXII 232

(Bite Sized Bake) 232

Chicken Breast XXIII 235

(Carrots, Peppers, and Parsley) 235

Chicken Breast XXIV 238

(Pineapple, Lime, and Garlic) 238

Chicken Breast XXV 241

(Parmesan, Spinach, and Pesto) 241

Chicken Breast XXVI 244
(Easy BBQ Style) 244
(Grilled) 244
Chicken Breast XXVII 247
(Stuffed IV) 247
(Crawfish, Crab, and Mushrooms) 247
Chicken Breast XXVIII.................. 251
(Coconut Cooked) 251
(Paleo Approved) 251
Chicken Breast XXVIII.................. 254
(Honey Mustard, Savory, and Mushrooms) 254
Chicken Breast XXX...................... 257
(Red Pepper, Cilantro, and Lime) . 257
Chicken Breast XXXI 260
(Stuffed V) 260
(Crab, Cream Cheese, and Garlic) . 260
Chicken Breast XXXII 263
(Stuffed VI) 263
(Bacon, Cornbread, and Jam) 263
Chicken Breast XXXIII 266

(Tarragon, Olives, and Lemon) 266

Chicken Breast XXXIV 269

(Stuffed VII) 269

(Peppers, Onions, Squash, and Cheddar) 269

Chicken Breast XXXV 272

(Easy Artisan Style) 272

Chicken Breast XXXVI 275

(Nutmeg, Almonds, and Mushrooms) 275

Chicken Breast XXXVII 278

(Sweet Potatoes and Balsamic) 278

Chicken Breast XXXVIII 281

(Creamy Raspberries and Shallots) 281

Chicken Breast XXXIX 284

(Lime and Chives) 284

Chicken Breast XL 287

(Maple Syrup and Pecans) 287

Chicken Breast XLI 290

(Easy Backroad Style) 290

Chicken Breast XLII 293

(Stuffed VIII) 293

(Apples and Cheddar) 293

Chicken Breast XLIII 296

(Buttery Capers and Lemon) 296

Chicken Breast XLIV 299

(Buttermilk and Honey) 299

Chicken Breast XLV 302

(Chili I) 302

Chicken Breast XLVI 306

(Restaurant Style II) 306

Chicken Breast XLVII 309

(Artisan Style II with Artichokes) .. 309

Chicken Breast XLVIII 312

(Stuffed IX) 312

(Honey Mustard, Brown Mustard, and Ham) 312

Chicken Breast XLIX 315

(Chili II) 315

Chicken Breast L 318

(Goat Cheese and Balsamic) 318

Chicken Thighs I 321

(Mandarin Chicken) 321
Chicken Thighs II 324
(Honey and Sriracha) 324
Chicken Thighs III 327
(Syrup and Sriracha) 327
Chicken Thighs IV 330
(Creamy Mushrooms and Onions) 330
Chicken Thighs V 333
(French Style and Apricots) 333
Chicken Thighs VI 335
(Dijon, Brown Sugar, and Cayenne)
.... 335
Chicken Thighs VII 339
(Onions, Carrots, and Rosemary) .. 339
Chicken Thighs VIII 342
(American Style I) 342
Chicken Thighs IX 345
(Indian Style I) 345
(Tandoori) 345
Chicken Thighs X 348
(Japanese Style I) 348

Chicken Thighs XI 351
(Honey Mustard and Curry) 351
Chicken Thighs XII 354
(Soy Sauce and Parsley) 354
Chicken Thighs XIII 357
(Red Potatoes and Parsley) 357
Chicken Thighs XIV 360
(Indian Style II) 360
(Makhani) 360
(Butter Chicken) 360
Chicken Thighs XV 364
(Mexican Fajitas) 364
Chicken Thighs XVI 367
(Fried and Baked) 367
Chicken Thighs XVII 370
(Japanese Style II) 370
Chicken Thighs XVIII 373
(Spanish Style) 373
Chicken Thighs XIX 376
(Soy Sauce, Honey, and Basil) 376

Chicken Thighs XX 378
(Maggie's Easy Sesame Chicken)... 378
Chicken Thighs XXI 382
(BBQ) 382
Chicken Thighs XXII 385
(Hawaiian Style) 385
Chicken Thighs XXIII 388
(Indian Style III) 388
(Makhani) 388
(Slow Cooker) 388
Chicken Thighs XXIV 391
(Arabic and Latin Fusion) 391
Chicken Thighs XXV 394
(Bacon and Potatoes) 394
Chicken Thighs XXVI 397
(Jalapenos, Peanuts, and Ginger) . 397
Chicken Thighs XXVII 400
(Buttery Mushroom Bake) 400
Chicken Thighs XXVIII 403
(Sunbelt Classic) 403

Chicken Thighs XXVIII 406
(Creamy Onions) 406
(Slow Cooker) 406
Chicken Thighs XXX 409
(Chicken and Rice) 409
Chicken Thighs XXXI 412
(Easy Sweet Bake) 412
Chicken Thighs XXXII 415
(Italian Style) 415
Chicken Thighs XXXIII 418
(Indian Style IV) 418
Chicken Thighs XXXIV 421
(Lemons and Oregano) 421
Chicken Thighs XXXV 424
(Buttery Garlic and Prosciutto) 424
Chicken Thighs XXXVI 427
(Louisiana Style) 427
(Gumbo) 427
Chicken Thighs XXXVII 431
(Thai Style) 431

Chicken Thighs XXXVIII 435

(Cream of Everything with Wine) . 435

Chicken Thighs XXXIX 438

(Moroccan Style) 438

(Tagine) 438

(Slow Cooker) 438

Chicken Thighs XL 442

(Italian Style II) 442

Chicken Thighs XLI 445

(Thai Style II) 445

Chicken Thighs XLII 448

(Creole Style I) 448

Chicken Thighs XLIII 451

(Thai Style III) 451

Chicken Thighs XLIV 454

(Chili Peppers and Monterey) 454

(Mexican Style) 454

Chicken Thighs XLV 457

(Vinegar and Salt) 457

(English Style) 457

Chicken Thighs XLVI 460
(Arabic Style) 460
Chicken Thighs XLVII.................... 463
(African Style)................................ 463
Chicken Thighs XLVIII 466
(Parsley, Peppers, and Sweet Onions)
.... 466
Chicken Thighs XLIX..................... 469
(Japanese Style III)........................ 469
Chicken Thighs L 472
(Cranberries and Onions) 472
EASY CHICKEN FRY........................... 475
GUMBO I 478
JAMBALAYA I 482
GUMBO II 485
JAMBALAYA II 489
JAMBALAYA III.................................. 492
CREOLE STYLE CHICKEN BREASTS 495
BOURBON CHICKEN 498
CAJUN GUMBO IV 501

Northeast Louisiana Style Cajun Wings with Sweet and Spicy Sauce 504

Bourbon Chicken II 507

Thanks for Reading! Now Let's Try some **Sushi** and **Dump Dinners**....
.... 510

Come On... 512

Let's Be Friends :) 512

Can I Ask A Favour? 513

Interested in Other Easy Cookbooks?
.... 514

Any Issues? Contact Me

If you find that something important to you is missing from this book please contact me at maggie@booksumo.com.

I will try my best to re-publish a revised copy taking your feedback into consideration and let you know when the book has been revised with you in mind.

:)

— Chef Maggie Chow

LEGAL NOTES

ALL RIGHTS RESERVED. NO PART OF THIS BOOK MAY BE REPRODUCED OR TRANSMITTED IN ANY FORM OR BY ANY MEANS. PHOTOCOPYING, POSTING ONLINE, AND / OR DIGITAL COPYING IS STRICTLY PROHIBITED UNLESS WRITTEN PERMISSION IS GRANTED BY THE BOOK'S PUBLISHING COMPANY. LIMITED USE OF THE BOOK'S TEXT IS PERMITTED FOR USE IN REVIEWS WRITTEN FOR THE PUBLIC AND/OR PUBLIC DOMAIN.

Common Abbreviations

cup(s)	C.
tablespoon	tbsp
teaspoon	tsp
ounce	oz.
pound	lb

*All units used are standard American measurements

Chapter 1: Easy Chicken Recipes

Tagine (Moroccan Style I)

Ingredients

- 2 tbsps olive oil
- 8 skinless, boneless chicken thighs, cut into 1-inch pieces
- 1 eggplant, cut into 1 inch cubes
- 2 large onions, thinly sliced
- 4 large carrots, thinly sliced
- 1/2 C. dried cranberries
- 1/2 C. chopped dried apricots
- 2 C. chicken broth
- 2 tbsps tomato paste
- 2 tbsps lemon juice
- 2 tbsps all-purpose flour
- 2 tsps garlic salt
- 1 1/2 tsps ground cumin

- 1 1/2 tsps ground ginger
- 1 tsp cinnamon
- 3/4 tsp ground black pepper
- 1 C. water
- 1 C. couscous

Directions

- Get a bowl, mix until smooth: black pepper, broth, cinnamon, tomato paste, ginger, flour, cumin, and garlic salt.
- Stir fry your chicken in olive oil until browned all over but still slightly uncooked.
- Now put the chicken into your crock pot along with the eggplant. Then add: apricots, onions, cranberries, and carrots.
- Add the broth mix too.
- For 5 hrs cook with the high setting.
- Now get a big pot and get your water boiling.

- Once it is boiling pour in your couscous.
- Get the mix boiling again, then place a lid on the pot and shut the heat.
- Let the couscous sit in the hot water for 7 mins. Then stir it.
- When the chicken is finished serve over the couscous.
- Enjoy.

Amount per serving (8 total)

Timing Information:

Preparation	Cooking	Total Time
30 m	5 h	5 h 30 m

Nutritional Information:

Calories	380 kcal
Fat	15.2 g
Carbohydrates	38.5g
Protein	22.3 g
Cholesterol	65 mg
Sodium	571 mg

* Percent Daily Values are based on a 2,000 calorie diet.

Couscous VIII

(Chicken, Cucumbers, and Parsley)

Ingredients

- 2 C. chicken broth
- 1 (10 oz.) box couscous
- 3/4 C. olive oil
- 1/4 C. fresh lemon juice
- 2 tbsps white balsamic vinegar
- 1/4 C. chopped fresh rosemary leaves
- salt and ground black pepper to taste
- 2 large cooked skinless, boneless chicken breast halves, cut into bite-size pieces
- 1 C. chopped English cucumber
- 1/2 C. chopped sun-dried tomatoes
- 1/2 C. chopped pitted kalamata olives
- 1/2 C. crumbled feta cheese

- 1/3 C. chopped fresh Italian parsley
- salt and ground black pepper to taste

Directions

- Get your stock boiling then add in your couscous.
- Place a lid on the pot and shut the heat.
- Let the contents sit for 7 mins before stirring.
- Blend: vinegar, olive oil, and lemon juice with some rosemary.
- Now add some pepper and salt before continuing.
- Get a bowl, mix: tomatoes, parsley, couscous, feta, cucumbers, and chicken.
- Cover the couscous with the dressing and add a bit more if you like also add some more pepper and salt too.
- Enjoy.

Amount per serving (6 total)

Timing Information:

Preparation	Cooking	Total Time
35 m	10 m	45 m

Nutritional Information:

Calories	645 kcal
Fat	38.8 g
Carbohydrates	44g
Protein	29.4 g
Cholesterol	68 mg
Sodium	792 mg

* Percent Daily Values are based on a 2,000 calorie diet.

Couscous IX

(Lime and Chicken)

Ingredients

- 1 tbsp olive oil
- 1 lb skinless, boneless chicken breast halves, cubed
- 1 pinch monosodium glutamate (MSG)
- 6 tbsps soy sauce
- 6 tbsps brown sugar
- 1/2 tsp red pepper flakes, or more to taste
- 1 lime, juiced and zested
- 2 C. vegetable broth
- 1 C. couscous
- 1/3 C. chopped cilantro
- 4 wedges lime for garnish

Directions

- Get a bowl, combine: zest, soy sauce, lime juice, sugar, and pepper flakes.
- Boil everything gently for 4 mins until it becomes sauce like.
- Now stir fry your chicken until it is fully done in olive oil for 7 mins.
- Add in your MSG while it fries.
- Then top everything with the lime sauce and continue stir frying for 4 more mins.
- Let your couscous sit in the veggie broth that was boiling for 7 mins in a covered pot.
- Place some couscous on a plate for serving and add a topping of lime chicken.
- Garnish with freshly squeezed lime from the wedges.
- Enjoy.

Amount per serving (4 total)

Timing Information:

Preparation	Cooking	Total Time
15 m	15 m	35 m

Nutritional Information:

Calories	380 kcal
Fat	6.2 g
Carbohydrates	52g
Protein	28.4 g
Cholesterol	59 mg
Sodium	1675 mg

* Percent Daily Values are based on a 2,000 calorie diet.

Couscous XIX

(Cloves, Onions, Tomatoes, and Chicken)

(Moroccan Style IV)

Ingredients

- 1 C. whole wheat couscous
- 1 tbsp vegetable oil
- 1 medium onion, chopped
- 2 bay leaves
- 5 whole cloves, crushed
- 1/2 tsp cinnamon
- 1 tsp ground dried turmeric
- 1/4 tsp ground cayenne pepper
- 6 skinless, boneless chicken breast halves - chopped
- 1 (16 oz.) can garbanzo beans
- 1 (16 oz.) can crushed tomatoes
- 1 (48 fluid oz.) can chicken broth
- 2 carrots, cut into 1/2 inch pieces

- 1 zucchini, cut into 1/2-inch pieces
- salt to taste

Directions

- Get your couscous boiling in water for 2 mins. Then place a lid on the pot, shut and heat, and it sit for 7 mins before stirring once it has cooled.
- Stir fry your onions in oil until soft then add in: cayenne, bay leaves, turmeric, cloves, and cinnamon.
- Cook everything for 1 more min then pour in your chicken and cook it until browned all over.
- Once everything has been browned add in: broth, tomatoes, and beans.
- Get everything boiling.
- Lower the heat to low and gently boil for 27 mins.
- Now add your zucchini and carrots and also some salt.

- Continue for 12 more mins.
- Serve the veggies and chicken over the couscous.
- Enjoy.

Amount per serving (6 total)

Timing Information:

Preparation	Cooking	Total Time
15 m	45 m	1 h

Nutritional Information:

Calories	399 kcal
Fat	6.7 g
Carbohydrates	50.7g
Protein	33.4 g
Cholesterol	67 mg
Sodium	1539 mg

* Percent Daily Values are based on a 2,000 calorie diet.

Couscous XXI

(Spicy Chicken and Carrots)

Ingredients

- 3 1/4 C. low-sodium chicken broth
- 1 C. quick-cooking couscous
- 2 tbsps olive oil
- 4 skinless, boneless chicken breast halves - cut into cubes
- 1 pinch ground black pepper
- 1/2 C. finely chopped jalapeno chili peppers
- 1 carrot, thinly sliced
- 1 zucchini, diced
- 3 green onions, thinly sliced
- 1 1/2 tsps grated fresh ginger root
- 1 1/2 tsps curry powder
- 1/2 tsp ground coriander seed
- 1 tsp cornstarch

Directions

- Boil your broth (2 C.) and then add the couscous and olive oil. Place a lid on the pot and let the contents sit for 12 mins.
- Get a bowl, mix: cornstarch, 1 C. of broth, and curry.
- Coat your chicken with pepper then stir fry it in 1 tbsp of olive oil until fully done.
- Remove the chicken from the pan.
- Add in more olive oil and stir fry carrots and jalapenos for 4 mins then add: a quarter of a C. of broth, zucchini, ginger, and onions.
- Cook everything for 7 more mins.
- Add your cornstarch mix and cook for 3 more mins.
- Serve the spicy chicken and carrots over the couscous.
- Enjoy.

Amount per serving (4 total)

Timing Information:

Preparation	Cooking	Total Time
20 m	25 m	45 m

Nutritional Information:

Calories	415 kcal
Fat	11.5 g
Carbohydrates	40.6g
Protein	35.8 g
Cholesterol	75 mg
Sodium	177 mg

* Percent Daily Values are based on a 2,000 calorie diet.

Couscous XXXIII

(Cucumbers, Capers, and Dates)

Ingredients

- 1 skinless, boneless chicken breast half
- 1/2 C. couscous
- 1/2 C. water
- 1 tbsp unsalted butter
- 1 pinch salt
- 1 tbsp salted butter
- 1/4 C. capers, drained
- 3 dates, pitted and chopped
- 1/4 C. mascarpone cheese
- 1/4 C. heavy cream
- salt and ground black pepper to taste (optional)
- 1 date, pitted and chopped
- 1/4 cucumber, diced
- 1/2 tomato, diced
- 1 tsp lemon juice (optional)

Directions

- Grill your chicken for 7 mins per side. Then divide it into two pieces.
- Boil your water with some salt and butter. Then pour in the couscous, place a lid on the pot, shut the heat to the stove, and let the contents sit for 12 mins.
- Let it cool and then stir it.
- Stir fry your dates and capers for a few mins in the butter then add in the cream and the cheese. Let the cheese mix cook for 4 mins.
- Place your couscous on serving platter add a diced date and then some cheese sauce and then the chicken.
- Add some chopped tomatoes and cucumber with some lemon juice as well.
- Enjoy.

Amount per serving (2 total)

Timing Information:

Preparation	Cooking	Total Time
30 m	25 m	55 m

Nutritional Information:

Calories	616 kcal
Fat	37.5 g
Carbohydrates	50.6g
Protein	21.9 g
Cholesterol	140 mg
Sodium	616 mg

* Percent Daily Values are based on a 2,000 calorie diet.

Couscous XXXV

(Carrots, Harissa, Peppers, Chicken, and Sausage)

Ingredients

- 3 tbsp olive oil
- 2 lbs chicken thighs
- 12 oz. Italian sausage
- 1 tbsp diced garlic
- 2 onions, minced
- 2 carrots, julienned
- 1/2 stalk celery, chunked
- 1 rutabaga, parsnip, or turnip, chunked
- 1/2 green bell pepper, julienned
- 1/2 red bell pepper, julienned
- 1 can diced tomatoes
- 1 can garbanzo beans
- 2 C. chicken stock
- 2 tsps thyme
- 1 tsp turmeric
- 1 tsp cayenne pepper

- 1/4 tsp harissa
- 1 bay leaf
- 2 zucchini, cut in half
- 2 C. couscous
- 2 C. chicken stock
- 1/2 C. plain yogurt

Directions

- Brown your chicken thighs all over in olive oil.
- Add in your sausage and cook everything until fully done. Once it has cooled dice the sausage into pieces.
- Now stir fry your garlic and onions until tender and see-through then combine in: stock, bay leaf, carrots, harissa, beans, celery, cayenne, tomatoes, turmeric, rutabaga, thyme, red and green peppers.
- Cook for 2 more mins before adding your chicken and sausage.

- Place a lid on the pan and cook for 35 mins until chicken is fully done.
- Add your zucchini and cook for 7 more mins.
- Meanwhile boil 2 C. of chicken stock then pour it over your couscous in a bowl along with 2 tbsps of olive oil.
- Place a covering on the bowl and let it sit for at least 10 mins.
- When plating the dish first layer couscous then some chicken mix and then some yogurt.
- Enjoy.

Amount per serving (6 total)

Timing Information:

Preparation	Cooking	Total Time
45 m	45 m	1 h 30 m

Nutritional Information:

Calories	934 kcal
Fat	39 g
Carbohydrates	80.5g
Protein	62.2 g
Cholesterol	169 mg
Sodium	601 mg

* Percent Daily Values are based on a 2,000 calorie diet.

Couscous XXXIX

(Tomatoes and Tarragon)

Ingredients

- 1 C. couscous
- 1 1/8 C. boiling chicken stock
- water to cover
- 2 tbsps butter
- 4 skinless, boneless chicken breast halves
- 2/3 C. heavy whipping cream
- 1/2 C. sweet corn
- 2 tomatoes, chopped
- 1/4 C. fresh chopped tarragon
- salt and pepper to taste
- 1/2 lemon, juiced

Directions

- Simmer for 4 mins, your couscous, in water and half of the stock.

- Shut the heat and place a lid on the pot.
- Stir fry your chicken in butter with the rest of the stock and cream until bubbly.
- Now add the tarragon, tomatoes, and corn, cook for 2 mins, before adding lemon juice, pepper and salt.
- Layer each plate with couscous and then the chicken mix.
- Enjoy.

Amount per serving (4 total)

Timing Information:

Preparation	Cooking	Total Time
10 m	30 m	40 m

Nutritional Information:

Calories	505 kcal
Fat	23.7 g
Carbohydrates	42.8g
Protein	30.8 g
Cholesterol	131 mg
Sodium	368 mg

* Percent Daily Values are based on a 2,000 calorie diet.

Chicken Adobo

Ingredients:

- 1 1/2 cups water
- 1 cup distilled white vinegar
- 4 tbsps soy sauce
- 1 tsp whole peppercorns
- 4 cloves garlic, crushed
- 2 tbsps salt
- 1 (2 to 3 pound) whole chicken, cut into pieces
- 2 tbsps vegetable oil

Directions:

- Mix water, salt, vinegar, peppercorns, garlic and soy sauce before adding chicken and cooking it over low heat for about 30 minutes or until the chicken is tender.
- Cook this chicken in hot oil until brown after removing it from the pot.

- Now put this chicken back into the pot and cook over medium heat until you see that the liquid has become thick.
- Serve.

Serving: 6

Timing Information:

Preparation	Cooking	Total Time
1 hr	15 mins	1 hr 15 mins

Nutritional Information:

Calories	340 kcal
Carbohydrates	2 g
Cholesterol	100 mg
Fat	21.5 g
Fiber	0.2 g
Protein	32.5 g
Sodium	3598 mg

* Percent Daily Values are based on a 2,000 calorie diet.

Chicken Mascarpone Pesto

Ingredients

- 6 slices bacon
- 2 tbsps olive oil
- 1 C. minced onion
- 3 lbs skinless, boneless chicken breast halves, cubed
- 1/2 tsp garlic powder
- salt and ground black pepper to taste
- 3 tbsps drained and chopped sun-dried tomatoes packed in oil
- 2 tbsps prepared pesto sauce
- 1/2 lb fresh spinach
- 1 (8 oz.) container mascarpone cheese
- 2 cloves garlic, minced
- 1 tbsp Dijon mustard, or more to taste
- 1 lemon, juiced
- 1/2 C. milk
- 1/4 tsp white pepper
- 1/2 C. grated Parmesan cheese

- 1 (16 oz.) package farfalle (bow tie) pasta
- 1 tbsp grated Parmesan cheese, or to taste

Directions

- Boil your pasta in water and salt for 9 mins. Then remove all the liquids.
- Fry your bacon for 11 mins.
- Then place it on some paper towel and break it into pieces.
- Add some olive oil to a new pot and then add the onions and bacon.
- Cook for 7 mins before adding the chicken and the following: black pepper, garlic powder, and salt.
- Now cook the chicken for 11 mins.
- Add the pesto and tomatoes and cook for 3 mins before adding in the spinach.
- Let the spinach wilt while stirring for 2 mins.

- Add the following to the spinach mix and stir fry for 7 mins: white pepper, cheese, milk, garlic, lemon juice, and Dijon.
- Now add the parmesan and cook for 3 mins.
- Get a bowl and add in the pasta as well as the chicken mix and toss everything evenly.
- Enjoy with a garnishing of more parmesan.

Amount per serving (8 total)

Timing Information:

Preparation	20 m
Cooking	40 m
Total Time	1 h

Nutritional Information:

Calories	637 kcal
Fat	28.2 g
Carbohydrates	46.9g
Protein	49.7 g
Cholesterol	138 mg
Sodium	448 mg

* Percent Daily Values are based on a 2,000 calorie diet.

Feta, Chicken, and Rosemary

(Greek Style Kebabs)

Ingredients

- 1 (8 oz.) container fat-free plain yogurt
- 1/3 C. crumbled feta cheese with basil and sun-dried tomatoes
- 1/2 tsp lemon zest
- 2 tbsps fresh lemon juice
- 2 tsps dried oregano
- 1/2 tsp salt
- 1/4 tsp ground black pepper
- 1/4 tsp crushed dried rosemary
- 1 lb. skinless, boneless chicken breast halves - cut into 1 inch pieces
- 1 large red onion, cut into wedges
- 1 large green bell pepper, cut into 1 1/2 inch pieces

Directions

- Get a bowl, combine: rosemary, yogurt, pepper, feta, salt, lemon zest, oregano, and lemon juice.
- Stir the contents until smooth then add in your chicken and stir everything again.
- Now place a covering of plastic around the bowl and putting everything in the fridge for 4 hrs.
- Get your grill hot and oil its grate.
- Stake your bell peppers, chicken, and onions onto skewers to form kebobs.
- Cook the kebobs on the grill until the chicken is fully done.
- Enjoy.

Amount per serving (4 total)

Timing Information:

Preparation	30 m
Cooking	15 m
Total Time	3 h 45 m

Nutritional Information:

Calories	243 kcal
Fat	7.5 g
Carbohydrates	12.3g
Protein	31 g
Cholesterol	85 mg
Sodium	632 mg

* Percent Daily Values are based on a 2,000 calorie diet.

Mediterranean Pasta

Ingredients

- 1 (16 oz.) package penne pasta
- 1 1/2 tbsps butter
- 1/2 C. chopped red onion
- 2 cloves garlic, minced
- 1 lb. skinless, boneless chicken breast halves - cut into bite-size pieces
- 1 (14 oz.) can artichoke hearts in water
- 1 tomato, chopped
- 1/2 C. crumbled feta cheese
- 3 tbsps chopped fresh parsley
- 2 tbsps lemon juice
- 1 tsp dried oregano
- salt to taste
- ground black pepper to taste

Directions

- Boil your pasta in water and salt for 9 mins then remove all the liquids.
- At the same time, stir fry your garlic and onions in butter for 4 mins, then combine in the chicken, and cook everything for 9 more mins.
- Set the heat to a low level and add in your artichokes after chopping them and discarding their liquids.
- Cook this mix for 3 more mins before adding in: pasta, tomatoes, oregano, feta, lemon juice, and the fresh parsley.
- Cook everything for 4 mins to get it all hot. Then add in your pepper and salt after shutting the heat.
- Enjoy.

Amount per serving (4 total)

Timing Information:

Preparation	20 m
Cooking	30 m
Total Time	50 m

Nutritional Information:

Calories	685 kcal
Fat	13.2 g
Carbohydrates	96.2g
Protein	47 g
Cholesterol	94 mg
Sodium	826 mg

* Percent Daily Values are based on a 2,000 calorie diet.

Chicken Souvlaki

Ingredients

Marinade:

- 3/4 C. balsamic vinaigrette salad dressing
- 3 tbsps lemon juice
- 1 tbsp dried oregano
- 1/2 tsp freshly ground black pepper
- 4 skinless, boneless chicken breast halves

White Sauce:

- 1/2 C. seeded, shredded cucumber
- 1 tsp kosher salt
- 1 C. plain yogurt
- 1/4 C. sour cream
- 1 tbsp lemon juice
- 1/2 tbsp rice vinegar

- 1 tsp olive oil
- 1 clove garlic, minced
- 1 tbsp chopped fresh dill
- 1/2 tsp Greek seasoning
- kosher salt to taste
- freshly ground black pepper to taste
- 4 large pita bread rounds
- 1 heart of romaine lettuce, cut into 1/4 inch slices
- 1 red onion, thinly sliced
- 1 tomato, halved and sliced
- 1/2 C. kalamata olives
- 1/2 C. pepperoncini
- 1 C. crumbled feta cheese

Directions

- Get a bowl, combine: chicken, black pepper (1/2 tsp), balsamic, oregano, and the juice of half of a lemon.
- Place a covering on the bowl and place the contents in the fridge for 2 hrs.

- Get a 2nd bowl and add in your cucumbers after shredding them and also some kosher salt.
- Let this stand for 10 mins.
- Get a 3rd bowl, combine: olive oil, garlic, yogurt, dill, rice vinegar, Greek seasoning, sour cream, and 1 tbsp of lemon juice.
- Place this mix in the fridge.
- Now grill your chicken pieces for 9 mins then flip them and cook the chicken pieces for 9 more mins.
- Let the chicken cool and then julienne it.
- Grill your pieces of pita for 3 mins and flip them throughout the entire grilling time.
- Fill each piece of pita with: pepperoncini, chicken, olive, lettuce, tomato, and onions.
- Add a topping of white sauce from the fridge and some feta on the side.
- Enjoy.

Amount per serving (4 total)

Timing Information:

Preparation	30 m
Cooking	20 m
Total Time	1 h 50 m

Nutritional Information:

Calories	764 kcal
Fat	40.5 g
Carbohydrates	55.9g
Protein	44.4 g
Cholesterol	133 mg
Sodium	3170 mg

* Percent Daily Values are based on a 2,000 calorie diet.

Easy Greek Style Chicken Breasts

Ingredients

- 2 tbsps all-purpose flour, divided
- 1/2 tsp salt
- 1/4 tsp black pepper
- 1/4 lb. feta cheese, crumbled
- 1 tbsp fresh lemon juice
- 1 tsp dried oregano
- 6 boneless, skinless chicken breast halves, flatten to 1/2 thickness
- 2 tbsps olive oil
- 1 1/2 C. water
- 1 cube chicken bouillon, crumbled
- 2 C. loosely packed torn fresh spinach leaves
- 1 ripe tomato, chopped

Directions

- Get a bowl, mix: oregano, cheese, and lemon juice.
- Get a 2nd bowl, combine: bouillon, 1 C. of water, and flour.
- Dredge you chicken in a mix of pepper, salt, and flour.
- Then fold each piece and stake a toothpick through each one.
- Sear the chicken in oil for 3 mins per side. Then top the chicken with the contents of the 2nd bowl.
- Cook everything for 1 more min before adding tomatoes and spinach.
- Get everything boiling and then place a lid on the pot.
- Set the heat to low and let it all cook for 12 mins.
- Enjoy.

Amount per serving (6 total)

Timing Information:

Preparation	20 m
Cooking	20 m
Total Time	40 m

Nutritional Information:

Calories	239 kcal
Fat	10.2 g
Carbohydrates	4.8g
Protein	31 g
Cholesterol	85 mg
Sodium	686 mg

* Percent Daily Values are based on a 2,000 calorie diet.

Chicken Soup

Ingredients

- 8 C. chicken broth
- 1/2 C. fresh lemon juice
- 1/2 C. shredded carrots
- 1/2 C. chopped onion
- 1/2 C. chopped celery
- 6 tbsps chicken soup base
- 1/4 tsp ground white pepper
- 1/4 C. margarine
- 1/4 C. all-purpose flour
- 1 C. cooked white rice
- 1 C. diced, cooked chicken meat
- 16 slices lemon
- 8 egg yolks

Directions

- Get the following boiling: white pepper, chicken broth, soup base, celery, lemon juice, onions, and carrots.

- Set the heat to low and let the contents cook for 23 mins.
- Begin heating the flour and butter while stirring and then add in the soup while continuing to stir and cook the mix for 12 more mins.
- Now start whisking your eggs and then add in some soup while continuing to whisk.
- Add the entire mix to your soup and also add the chicken and the rice.
- When serving the soup top it with some pieces of lemon.
- Enjoy.

Amount per serving (16 total)

Timing Information:

Preparation	25 m
Cooking	40 m
Total Time	1 h 5 m

Nutritional Information:

Calories	124 kcal
Fat	6.6 g
Carbohydrates	9.1g
Protein	7.8 g
Cholesterol	110 mg
Sodium	1237 mg

* Percent Daily Values are based on a 2,000 calorie diet.

Easiest Greek Chicken

Ingredients

- 4 skinless, boneless chicken breast halves
- 1 C. extra virgin olive oil
- 1 lemon, juiced
- 2 tsps crushed garlic
- 1 tsp salt
- 1 1/2 tsps black pepper
- 1/3 tsp paprika

Directions

- Slice a few incisions into your pieces of chicken before doing anything else.
- Now get a bowl, combine: paprika, olive oil, pepper, lemon juice, salt, and garlic.
- Now add in the chicken and place the contents in the fridge for 8 hrs.

- Grill your chicken until fully done with indirect heat on the side of the grill with the grilling grates oiled.
- Enjoy.

Amount per serving (4 total)

Timing Information:

Preparation	10 m
Cooking	8 h
Total Time	8 h 30 m

Nutritional Information:

Calories	644 kcal
Fat	57.6 g
Carbohydrates	4g
Protein	27.8 g
Cholesterol	68 mg
Sodium	660 mg

* Percent Daily Values are based on a 2,000 calorie diet.

Chicken Souvlaki II

Ingredients

- 1/4 C. olive oil
- 2 tbsps lemon juice
- 2 cloves garlic, minced
- 1 tsp dried oregano
- 1/2 tsp salt
- 1 1/2 lbs skinless, boneless chicken breast halves - cut into bite-sized pieces
- Sauce:
- 1 (6 oz.) container plain Greek-style yogurt
- 1/2 cucumber - peeled, seeded, and grated
- 1 tbsp olive oil
- 2 tsps white vinegar
- 1 clove garlic, minced
- 1 pinch salt
- 6 wooden skewers, or as needed

Directions

- Take your skewers and submerge them in water before doing anything else.
- Get a bowl, mix: half tsp salt, quarter of a C. of olive oil, chicken, oregano, lemon juice, and 2 cloves of garlic.
- Place a covering on the bowl and put it all in the fridge for 3 hrs.
- Get a 2nd bowl, combine: some salt, yogurt, 1 piece of garlic, 1 tbsp of olive oil, and the cucumbers.
- Place this in the fridge for 3 hrs as well.
- Stake your chicken on the skewers and then grill them for 9 mins, turn them over and cook for 8 more mins.
- Top the chicken with the white sauce.
- Enjoy.

Amount per serving (6 total)

Timing Information:

Preparation	15 m
Cooking	15 m
Total Time	2 h 30 m

Nutritional Information:

Calories	268 kcal
Fat	16.8 g
Carbohydrates	2.6g
Protein	< 25.5 g
Cholesterol	71 mg
Sodium	295 mg

* Percent Daily Values are based on a 2,000 calorie diet.

Indonesian Classical Satay

Ingredients

- 3 tbsps soy sauce
- 3 tbsps tomato sauce
- 1 tbsp peanut oil
- 2 cloves garlic, peeled and minced
- 1 pinch ground black pepper
- 1 pinch ground cumin
- 6 skinless, boneless chicken breast halves - cubed
- 1 tbsp vegetable oil
- 1/4 cup minced onion
- 1 clove garlic, peeled and minced
- 1 cup water
- 1/2 cup chunky peanut butter
- 2 tbsps soy sauce
- 2 tbsps white sugar
- 1 tbsp lemon juice
- skewers

Directions

- At first you need to set a grill or grilling plate to high heat and put some oil before starting anything else.
- Coat chicken with a mixture of soy sauce, cumin, tomato sauce, black pepper, peanut oil and garlic, and refrigerate it for at least 15 minutes.
- Cook onion and garlic in hot oil until brown before adding water, sugar, peanut butter and soy sauce into it.
- Add lemon juice after removing from heat.
- Thread all the chicken pieces into skewers
- Cook this on the preheated grill for about 5 minutes each side or until tender.
- Serve this with peanut sauce.

NOTE: If using a grilling plate please adjust the cooking time of the meat, to make sure that everything is cooked fully through.

Serving: 6

Timing Information:

Preparation	Cooking	Total Time
25 mins	20 mins	1 hr

Nutritional Information:

Calories	329 kcal
Carbohydrates	11.8 g
Cholesterol	67 mg
Fat	18.2 g
Fiber	2.2 g
Protein	30.8 g
Sodium	957 mg

* Percent Daily Values are based on a 2,000 calorie diet.

Satay Ayam

(Indo chicken with Peanut Sauce)

Ingredients

- 1 pound chicken thighs, cut into 1/2-inch pieces
- 3/4 tsp salt
- 1 pinch ground white pepper
- 1 tbsp sunflower seed oil
- 24 wooden skewers

Peanut Sauce:

- 1 cup water
- 5 tbsps peanut butter
- 2 tbsps kecap manis (sweet soy sauce)
- 1 tbsp brown sugar
- 2 cloves garlic, minced
- 1/2 tsp salt
- 1 tbsp lime juice

Directions

- Coat chicken thighs with ¾ tsp salt, sunflower seed oil and white pepper before refrigerating it for at least two hours.
- Bring a mixture of water, salt, peanut butter, kecap manis, garlic and brown sugar to boil before removing it from heat and adding some lime juice to make peanut sauce.
- Thread these chicken thighs onto skewers, while saving some marinade for later use.
- Cook these chicken thighs on a preheated grill for about 2 minutes each side or until tender.
- Serve this with peanut sauce.

NOTE: To make kecap manis, boil the following for 30 mins: 2/3 cup soy sauce, 1 cup water, 2/3 cup brown sugar, and 8 bay leaves. After you finish boiling the mix discard the leaves and let the sauce cool.

Serving: 4

Timing Information:

Preparation	Cooking	Total Time
10 mins	30 mins	40 mins

Nutritional Information:

Calories	326 kcal
Carbohydrates	8.9 g
Cholesterol	70 mg
Fat	21.8 g
Fiber	1.4 g
Protein	24.9 g
Sodium	1339 mg

* Percent Daily Values are based on a 2,000 calorie diet.

Chicken & Broccoli

Ingredients

- 12 ounces boneless, skinless chicken breast halves, cut into bite-sized pieces
- 1 tbsp oyster sauce
- 2 tbsps dark soy sauce
- 3 tbsps vegetable oil
- 2 cloves garlic, chopped
- 1 large onion, cut into rings
- 1/2 cup water
- 1 tsp ground black pepper
- 1 tsp white sugar
- 1/2 medium head bok choy, chopped
- 1 small head broccoli, chopped
- 1 tbsp cornstarch, mixed with equal parts water

Directions

- Mix chicken, soy sauce and oyster sauce in large bowl and set it aside for later use.
- Cook garlic and onion in hot oil for about three minutes before adding chicken mixture and cooking it for another ten minutes.
- Now add water, sugar, broccoli, pepper and bok choy, and cook it for another ten minutes.
- In the end, add cornstarch mixture and cook it for another 5 minutes to get the sauce thick.
- Enjoy.

Serving: 6

Timing Information:

Preparation	Cooking	Total Time
10 mins	25 mins	35 mins

Nutritional Information:

Calories	170 kcal
Carbohydrates	9.8 g
Cholesterol	33 mg
Fat	7.9 g
Fiber	2.5 g
Protein	16.2 g
Sodium	418 mg

* Percent Daily Values are based on a 2,000 calorie diet.

Chicken Wings in Japan

(鶏手羽肉)

Ingredients

- 3 pounds chicken wings
- 1 egg, lightly beaten
- 1 cup all-purpose flour for coating
- 1 cup butter

SAUCE

- 3 tbsps soy sauce
- 3 tbsps water
- 1 cup white sugar
- 1/2 cup white vinegar
- 1/2 tsp garlic powder, or to taste
- 1 tsp salt

Directions

- Get your oven to 350 degrees before doing anything else.
- Slice your wings into two pieces. Get two bowls: one with egg, another with flour.
- Coat the wings with egg first, then flour.
- Get a frying pan and get butter melted.

- Fry wings until completely golden brown.
- Then move the wings into a saucepan.
- Get a bowl mix the following: salt, soy sauce, garlic powder, water, vinegar, and sugar. Use to coat wings.
- Enter wings into the oven for 40 mins. Make sure to baste with remaining wet mixture occasionally.
- Enjoy.

Servings: 6 servings

Timing Information:

Preparation	Cooking	Total Time
15 mins	45 mins	1 hr

Nutritional Information:

Calories	675 kcal
Carbohydrates	51.4 g
Cholesterol	158 mg
Fat	44.3 g
Fiber	0.7 g
Protein	18.9 g
Sodium	1112 mg

Percent Daily Values are based on a 2,000 calorie diet.

Fried Chicken

(フライドチキン)

Ingredients

- 2 eggs, lightly beaten
- 1/2 tsp salt
- 1/2 tsp black pepper
- 1/2 tsp white sugar
- 1 tbsp minced garlic
- 1 tbsp grated fresh ginger root
- 1 tbsp sesame oil
- 1 tbsp soy sauce
- 1/8 tsp chicken bouillon granules
- 1 1/2 pounds skinless, boneless chicken breast halves - cut into 1 inch cubes
- 3 tbsps potato starch
- 1 tbsp rice flour
- oil for frying

Directions

- Get a bowl and combine the following: bouillon, eggs, soy sauce, salt, sesame oil, pepper, ginger, garlic, and sugar. Use as a marinade for the chicken. Place a

lid over the contents. And let the chicken marinate in this mixture at least 35 mins in the frig.
- Take off the lid from the marinade and add rice flour and potato starch to it. Evenly combine everything.
- Get a frying pan and get oil to 365 degrees.
- Fry your chicken until brown in a batch process.
- Remove excess oil.
- Enjoy.

Servings: 8 servings

Timing Information:

Preparation	Cooking	Total Time
20 mins	20 mins	1 hr 10 mins

Nutritional Information:

Calories	256 kcal
Carbohydrates	4.8 g
Cholesterol	98 mg
Fat	16.7 g
Fiber	0.1 g
Protein	20.9 g
Sodium	327 mg

* Percent Daily Values are based on a 2,000 calorie diet.

Katsu

Ingredients

- 4 skinless, boneless chicken breast halves - pounded to 1/2 inch thickness
- salt and pepper to taste
- 2 tbsps all-purpose flour
- 1 egg, beaten
- 1 cup panko bread crumbs
- 1 cup oil for frying, or as needed

Directions

- Get three bowls. Bowl 1 for chicken with some pepper and salt. Bowl 2 for bread crumbs. Bowl 3 for eggs.
- Cover chicken with flour first. Then with egg, and finally with crumbs.
- Get a frying pan and heat 1/4 inch of oil. Fry your chicken for 5 mins on each side.
- Remove excess oil.
- Enjoy.

Servings: 4 servings

Timing Information:

Preparation	Cooking	Total Time
10 mins	10 mins	20 mins

Nutritional Information:

Calories	297 kcal
Carbohydrates	22.2 g
Cholesterol	118 mg
Fat	11.4 g
Fiber	0.1 g
Protein	31.2 g
Sodium	251 mg

* Percent Daily Values are based on a 2,000 calorie diet.

Tak Toritang

(Potato and Chicken)

Ingredients

- 2 1/2 lbs chicken drumettes
- 2 large potatoes, cut into large chunks
- 2 carrots, cut into 2 inch pieces
- 1 large onion, cut into 8 pieces
- 4 cloves garlic, crushed
- 1/4 C. water
- 1/2 C. soy sauce
- 2 tbsps white sugar
- 3 tbsps hot pepper paste

Directions

- Get the following boiling in a big pot: hot pepper paste, potatoes, sugar, carrots, soy sauce, water, onions, and garlic.

- Once it is all boiling set the heat to its lowest level and cook the mix for 50 mins.
- At this point the liquid should be thick.
- Enjoy.

Amount per serving (4 total)

Timing Information:

Preparation	Cooking	Total Time
15 m	45 m	1 h

Nutritional Information:

Calories	447 kcal
Fat	14.1 g
Carbohydrates	54.7g
Protein	25.7 g
Cholesterol	60 mg
Sodium	1994 mg

* Percent Daily Values are based on a 2,000 calorie diet.

Korean Teriyaki

Ingredients

- 1/4 C. soy sauce
- 1 C. water
- 1/3 C. maple syrup
- 3 tbsps dark sesame oil
- 2 cloves garlic, crushed
- 1 tbsp minced fresh ginger root
- 2 tsps ground black pepper
- 5 skinless, boneless chicken breast halves
- 1 C. brown rice
- 2 C. water
- 2 tbsps cornstarch

Directions

- Get a bowl, combine: pepper, soy sauce, ginger, 1 C. of water, garlic, maple syrup, and sesame oil.
- Reserve 1/3 of a C. of the mix and then add in your chicken.

- Stir the chicken in the marinade and place a covering of plastic around the bowl.
- Put everything in the fridge for 3 hrs.
- Get your rice and 2 C. of water boiling.
- Once it is boiling, set the heat to its lowest level, place a lid on the pot, and let the rice cook for 50 mins.
- Coat a casserole dish with oil and then turn on your oven's broiler before doing anything else.
- Put your chicken pieces in the casserole dish and then begin to boil the associated marinade.
- Add in some cornstarch and stir the mix while it is boiling and continue heating until it is thick.
- At the same time cook your chicken for 9 mins each side under the broiler and baste the meat with the marinade.
- Enjoy.

Amount per serving (5 total)

Timing Information:

Preparation	Cooking	Total Time
15 m	1 h	3 h 15 m

Nutritional Information:

Calories	388 kcal
Fat	11.9 g
Carbohydrates	41.5g
Protein	27.7 g
Cholesterol	67 mg
Sodium	785 mg

* Percent Daily Values are based on a 2,000 calorie diet.

Bulgogi II

(Korean Chicken Stir Fry)

Ingredients

- 1/4 C. diced onion
- 5 tbsps soy sauce
- 2 1/2 tbsps brown sugar
- 2 tbsps minced garlic
- 2 tbsps sesame oil
- 1 tbsp sesame seeds
- 1/2 tsp cayenne
- salt and ground black pepper to taste
- 1 lb skinless, boneless chicken breasts, cut into thin strips

Directions

- Get a bowl, combine: black pepper, onions, salt, brown sugar, soy sauce, cayenne, garlic, sesame seeds, and sesame oils.

- Add in your chicken to the mix and stir the mix before pouring everything in a wok.
- Stir fry the contents until your chicken is fully done for about 17 mins.
- Enjoy.

Amount per serving (4 total)

Timing Information:

Preparation	Cooking	Total Time
15 m	15 m	30 m

Nutritional Information:

Calories	269 kcal
Fat	11.6 g
Carbohydrates	13.2g
Protein	27.5 g
Cholesterol	69 mg
Sodium	1230 mg

* Percent Daily Values are based on a 2,000 calorie diet.

Chicken from Korea

Ingredients

- 1 (3 lb) whole chicken, meat remove from the bones, slices in the 1/8" thick square pieces
- 1/4 C. soy sauce
- 2 tbsps sesame seeds
- 1/8 tsp salt
- 1/8 tsp ground black pepper
- 1 green onion, minced
- 1 clove garlic, minced
- 1 tsp peanut oil
- 1 tbsp white sugar
- 1 tsp monosodium glutamate (MSG)

Directions

- Combine your cut chicken with some soy sauce in a bowl.
- Now toast your sesame seeds in a pan.

- Once they begin to pop place them in a bowl and top the seeds with salt.
- Now mash the seeds with a big wooden spoon and add in: MSG, pepper, sugar, onions, oil, and garlic.
- Now combine both bowls and let the chicken sit in the sesame mix for 35 mins.
- Begin to stir fry your chicken in the same pan for 2 mins before placing a cover on the pot and cooking until the meat is fully done.
- Enjoy.

Amount per serving (4 total)

Timing Information:

Preparation	Cooking	Total Time
10 m	40 m	50 m

Nutritional Information:

Calories	794 kcal
Fat	54.7 g
Carbohydrates	6g
Protein	65.3 g
Cholesterol	1255 mg
Sodium	1338 mg

* Percent Daily Values are based on a 2,000 calorie diet.

Korean Chicken Stew

Ingredients

- 1 1/2 C. water
- 1/4 C. soy sauce
- 2 tbsps rice wine
- 2 tbsps Korean red chili pepper paste (gochujang)
- 2 tbsps Korean red chili pepper flakes (gochugaru)
- 1 tbsp honey
- 1 tbsp white sugar
- 1 pinch ground black pepper
- 3 lbs bone-in chicken pieces, trimmed of fat and cut into small pieces
- 10 oz. potatoes, cut into large chunks
- 2 carrots, cut into large chunks
- 1/2 large onion, cut into large chunks
- 4 large garlic cloves, or more to taste

- 2 slices fresh ginger, or more to taste
- 2 scallions, cut into 2-inch lengths
- 1 tbsp sesame oil
- 1 tsp sesame seeds

Directions

- Get the following boiling in a big pot: chicken, water, black pepper, soy sauce, sugar, wine, honey, pepper paste, and pepper flakes.
- Once everything is boiling set the heat to low and place a lid on the pot.
- Let the contents cook for 17 mins.
- Add in: ginger, potatoes, garlic, carrots, and onions and cook the mix for 17 more mins.
- Take off the lid and continue cooking for 12 more mins.
- Now add in some sesame seeds, scallions, and sesame oil.
- Enjoy.

Amount per serving (4 total)

Timing Information:

Preparation	Cooking	Total Time
20 m	45 m	1 h 5 m

Nutritional Information:

Calories	896 kcal
Fat	69.1 g
Carbohydrates	136.1g
Protein	33.4 g
Cholesterol	121 mg
Sodium	1111 mg

* Percent Daily Values are based on a 2,000 calorie diet.

Chili II

(Chicken, Peppers, and Jalapenos)

Ingredients

- 2 (10 oz.) cans chunk chicken, undrained
- 2 (16 oz.) cans chili beans, drained
- 3 (14.5 oz.) cans Mexican-style stewed tomatoes
- 1 (12 oz.) jar sliced jalapeno peppers
- 1 large onion, diced
- 2 large green bell peppers, seeded and diced
- 1 1/2 tbsps chili powder
- 2 tbsps ground cumin
- 10 C. water, or as needed
- 1 (14.5 oz.) can chicken broth
- salt to taste

Directions

- Get a big saucepan and add in: broth, chicken, cumin, beans, chili powder, tomatoes, bell peppers, jalapenos, and onions. Add in your water as well then get everything boiling.
- Once the mix is boiling set the heat to a medium level and let the contents gently boil for at least 65 mins.
- Add in your preferred amount of additional pepper and salt.
- Enjoy.

Amount per serving (15 total)

Timing Information:

Preparation	30 m
Cooking	1 h 15 m
Total Time	1 h 45 m

Nutritional Information:

Calories	149 kcal
Fat	4 g
Carbohydrates	18.8g
Protein	12.7 g
Cholesterol	23 mg
Sodium	714 mg

* Percent Daily Values are based on a 2,000 calorie diet.

Chili V

(Rustic)

Ingredients

- 4 skinless, boneless chicken breast halves
- 1 (16 oz.) jar salsa
- 2 tsps garlic powder
- 1 tsp ground cumin
- 1 tsp chili powder
- salt to taste
- ground black pepper to taste
- 1 (11 oz.) can Mexican-style corn
- 1 (15 oz.) can pinto beans

Directions

- Get a bowl, mix: chicken, pepper, garlic powder, salt, chili powder, and cumin.

- Now cook your salsa and chicken for 7 hours with a low heat in the slow cooker.
- After the meat has cooked for 4 hours take it out of the slow cooker and shred it.
- Place it back in the crock pot along with the beans and corn and continue cooking.
- Enjoy.

Amount per serving (6 total)

Timing Information:

Preparation	15 m
Cooking	12 h
Total Time	12 h 15 m

Nutritional Information:

Calories	188 kcal
Fat	2.3 g
Carbohydrates	22.6g
Protein	20.4 g
Cholesterol	41 mg
Sodium	1012 mg

* Percent Daily Values are based on a 2,000 calorie diet.

Chili X

(White Beans)

Ingredients

- 1 tbsp vegetable oil
- 1 onion, diced
- 3 cloves garlic, crushed
- 1 (4 oz.) can diced jalapeno peppers
- 1 (4 oz.) can diced green chili peppers
- 2 tsps ground cumin
- 1 tsp dried oregano
- 1 tsp ground cayenne pepper
- 2 (14.5 oz.) cans chicken broth
- 3 C. diced cooked chicken breast
- 3 (15 oz.) cans white beans
- 1 C. shredded Monterey Jack cheese

Directions

- Stir fry your onions until soft, in oil, then add in, cayenne, garlic, oregano, jalapenos, cumin, and chili peppers.
- Cook this mix for 4 more mins then pour in the beans, chicken, and broth.
- Get everything boiling then set the heat to low and simmer the contents for 17 mins.
- Stir the chili every 4 mins.
- Shut the heat and add the cheese.
- Once the cheese has melted, your chili is ready to serve.
- Enjoy.

Amount per serving (4 total)

Timing Information:

Preparation	10 m
Cooking	20 m
Total Time	30 m

Nutritional Information:

Calories	684 kcal
Fat	16.8 g
Carbohydrates	74.9g
Protein	59.1 g
Cholesterol	1102 mg
Sodium	1896 mg

* Percent Daily Values are based on a 2,000 calorie diet.

Chili XII

(White Beans and Tomatillos)

Ingredients

- 2 tbsps vegetable oil
- 1 onion, diced
- 2 cloves garlic, minced
- 1 (14.5 oz.) can chicken broth
- 1 (18.75 oz.) can tomatillos, drained and diced
- 1 (16 oz.) can diced tomatoes
- 1 (7 oz.) can diced green chilis
- 1/2 tsp dried oregano
- 1/2 tsp ground coriander seed
- 1/4 tsp ground cumin
- 2 ears fresh corn
- 1 lb diced, cooked chicken meat
- 1 (15 oz.) can white beans
- 1 pinch salt and black pepper to taste

Directions

- Stir fry your garlic and onions in oil for about 7 mins until they are tender then add in: spices, broth, chilies and tomatillos, and the tomatoes.
- Get the mix boiling and then lower the height to a light boil.
- Let the mix gently boil for 12 mins. Then add in: beans, chicken and corn.
- Continue cooking for 10 more mins.
- Add in your preferred amount of pepper and salt and then let the chili cool before serving.
- Enjoy.

Amount per serving (9 total)

Timing Information:

Preparation	10 m
Cooking	25 m
Total Time	35 m

Nutritional Information:

Calories	220 kcal
Fat	6.1 g
Carbohydrates	21.2g
Protein	20.1 g
Cholesterol	40 mg
Sodium	786 mg

* Percent Daily Values are based on a 2,000 calorie diet.

Asparagus XI

(Red Peppers, Mozzarella, and Chicken)

Ingredients

- 1/2 C. chicken broth
- 1 lb. boned and skinned chicken breast halves
- salt and pepper to taste
- 1/2 lb. fresh asparagus, trimmed and cut into 2 inch pieces
- 1 (7 oz.) jar roasted red peppers, drained and chopped1 clove garlic, minced
- 1/2 C. chopped roma (plum) tomatoes
- 1 tsp balsamic vinegar, or to taste
- 1/2 C. shredded mozzarella cheese

Directions

- Coat your chicken with pepper and salt and add it to a pot with the broth.
- Cook everything for 17 mins until the chicken is basically done.
- Then add: garlic, asparagus, and peppers and cook the mix for 11 more mins.
- Add in your tomatoes and heat for 4 more mins before adding in vinegar and cooking for 2 mins.
- Top the dish with mozzarella.
- Enjoy.

Amount per serving (4 total)

Timing Information:

Preparation	15 m
Cooking	25 m
Total Time	40 m

Nutritional Information:

Calories	184 kcal
Fat	5 g
Carbohydrates	6.5g
Protein	27.6 g
Cholesterol	68 mg
Sodium	316 mg

* Percent Daily Values are based on a 2,000 calorie diet.

Asparagus V

(Tarragon, Lemons, and Provolone)

Ingredients

- 1/2 C. mayonnaise
- 3 tbsps Dijon mustard
- 1 lemon, juiced and zested
- 2 tsps dried tarragon
- 1 tsp ground black pepper
- 1/2 tsp salt
- 16 spears fresh asparagus, trimmed
- 4 skinless, boneless chicken breast halves
- 4 slices provolone cheese
- 1 C. panko bread crumbs

Directions

- Coat a casserole dish with oil and then set your oven to 475 degrees before doing anything else.
- Get a bowl, combine the following until smooth: pepper, mayo, salt, Dijon, tarragon, lemon zest, and juice.
- Microwave your asparagus for 2 mins.
- Now flatten your chicken breasts with a mallet to a quarter of an inch.
- Put a piece of cheese on each piece of chicken and also four pieces of asparagus.
- Now roll the chicken breast around the asparagus.
- Put the rolls into the dish and then top with some Dijon mix and some bread crumbs.
- Cook the chicken in the fridge for 27 mins and the chicken is fully done.
- Enjoy.

Amount per serving (4 total)

Timing Information:

Preparation	25 m
Cooking	30 m
Total Time	55 m

Nutritional Information:

Calories	530 kcal
Fat	33.3 g
Carbohydrates	28.8g
Protein	36.8 g
Cholesterol	97 mg
Sodium	1170 mg

* Percent Daily Values are based on a 2,000 calorie diet.

Asparagus VI

(Parmesan and Penne)

Ingredients

- 1 (16 oz.) package dried penne pasta
- 5 tbsps olive oil, divided
- 2 skinless, boneless chicken breast halves - cut into cubes
- salt and pepper to taste
- garlic powder to taste1/2 C. low-sodium chicken broth
- 1 bunch slender asparagus spears, trimmed, cut on diagonal into 1-inch pieces
- 1 clove garlic, thinly sliced
- 1/4 C. Parmesan cheese

Directions

- Boil your pasta in salt and water for 9 mins. The remove all the liquid.
- Coat your chicken with garlic powder, pepper, and salt before frying them in olive oil (3 tbsps) for 7 mins. Place everything on paper towels to remove excess oils.
- Add the broth to the pan and then add: pepper, asparagus, salt, garlic, and garlic powder.
- Cook the asparagus with a lid on the pan for 8 mins. Then add in your chicken and heat it up again.
- Add the pasta to the pan and let everything rest for 7 mins. Add in parmesan and 2 tbsps of olive oil before serving.
- Enjoy.

Amount per serving (8 total)

Timing Information:

Preparation	15 m
Cooking	20 m
Total Time	35 m

Nutritional Information:

Calories	332 kcal
Fat	10.9 g
Carbohydrates	43.3g
Protein	16.7 g
Cholesterol	20 mg
Sodium	69 mg

* Percent Daily Values are based on a 2,000 calorie diet.

Asparagus XVI

(Chicken Stuffed)

Ingredients

- 2 large skinless, boneless chicken breast halves
- salt and black pepper to taste
- 8 asparagus spears, trimmed - divided
- 1/2 C. shredded mozzarella cheese, divided
- 1/4 C. Italian seasoned bread crumbs

Directions

- Oil a casserole dish or apply a coating of nonstick spray before setting your oven to 375 degrees before doing anything else.

- Flatten your chicken to a quarter of an inch and then coat it with pepper and salt.
- Put 4 pieces of asparagus in the center of each chicken breast and a quarter of your cheese.
- Roll up the chicken and place them in the casserole dish evenly.
- Top each piece with an equal amount of bread crumbs and cook everything in the oven for 27 to 30 mins.
- Enjoy.

Amount per serving (2 total)

Timing Information:

Preparation	20 m
Cooking	25 m
Total Time	45 m

Nutritional Information:

Calories	390 kcal
Fat	10.8 g
Carbohydrates	13.3g
Protein	57.4 g
Cholesterol	1147 mg
Sodium	581 mg

* Percent Daily Values are based on a 2,000 calorie diet.

Asparagus XXIV

(Asian Stir Fry)

Ingredients

- 1 whole boneless, skinless chicken breast, cubed
- 2 C. wild rice, cooked
- 1/2 lb. fresh asparagus
- 3 tbsps hoisin sauce
- 4 tbsps peanut oil
- 1 tbsp brown sugar

Directions

- Cut your asparagus into pieces. Then place everything in a bowl and mix in: brown sugar, and hoisin.
- Now cook your rice.
- Place the rice into boiling water, then place a lid on the pan, set

the heat to low, and simmer for 22 mins.
- In a wok stir fry your asparagus in 1 tbsp of oil for 3 mins, and then take it out of the pan.
- Increase the heat and add in 2 more tbsps of oil and cook the chicken until fully done.
- Place the asparagus back into the pot and add in the reserved liquid.
- Stir the contents over heat for 2 mins.
- Enjoy with your rice.

Amount per serving (2 total)

Timing Information:

Preparation	20 m
Cooking	10 m
Total Time	30 m

Nutritional Information:

Calories	635 kcal
Fat	30 g
Carbohydrates	56.6g
Protein	37.1 g
Cholesterol	69 mg
Sodium	473 mg

* Percent Daily Values are based on a 2,000 calorie diet.

Asparagus XXVI

(Thai Style)

Ingredients

- 2 C. dry jasmine rice
- 3 C. water
- 1 1/2 lb. skinless, boneless chicken breast halves - cubed
- 1 tbsp curry powder
- 2 C. 1 inch pieces asparagus
- 1 C. snow peas
- 1/2 C. shredded carrots
- 1 C. chopped green onions
- 1 (14 oz.) can light coconut milk

Directions

- Get a large pan and boil your water in it.
- Once it is boiling pour in your rice and get it all boiling again.

- Now place a lid on the pot, and let the rice cook for 22 mins with a low heat.
- Get a bowl, mix: curry powder, and chicken.
- Stir fry your chicken in a wok coated with nonstick spray for 5 mins then add: green onions, asparagus, carrots, and snow peas.
- Continue stir frying for 4 mins then add in the coconut milk and continue cooking for 3 more mins while stirring.
- Enjoy the chicken and milk over warm rice.

Amount per serving (4 total)

Timing Information:

Preparation	10 m
Cooking	20 m
Total Time	30 m

Nutritional Information:

Calories	697 kcal
Fat	12.1 g
Carbohydrates	91.4g
Protein	50.9 g
Cholesterol	199 mg
Sodium	141 mg

* Percent Daily Values are based on a 2,000 calorie diet.

Dumplings

Ingredients

- 3 slices bacon
- 3 large potatoes, peeled and diced
- 1 onion, diced
- 4 skinless, boneless chicken breast halves - diced
- 3 C. chicken broth
- 1 tsp poultry seasoning
- salt and pepper to taste
- 1 (15.25 oz.) can whole kernel corn, drained and rinsed
- 3 C. half-and-half
- 1 1/2 C. biscuit mix
- 1 C. milk

Directions

- Fry your bacon and then break the bacon into pieces and place the bacon pieces to the side.

- For 17 mins cook the following in the bacon drippings: chicken (coated with poultry seasoning), salt, onions, pepper, and potatoes.
- Now add the corn and broth and get everything to a light boil with a low level of heat. Continue cooking for 14 more mins.
- Add the half and half and get everything boiling again.
- Once it is all boiling add in the bacon.
- Get a bowl, mix: milk and biscuit powder.
- Form a dough from this mixture and add dollops of the dough into the broth.
- Cook everything for 12 mins with a lid on the pot and a low level of heat and no stirring.
- Enjoy.

Amount per serving (8 total)

Timing Information:

Preparation	20 m
Cooking	30 m
Total Time	50 m

Nutritional Information:

Calories	457 kcal
Fat	21 g
Carbohydrates	44.6g
Protein	23.8 g
Cholesterol	80 mg
Sodium	1005 mg

* Percent Daily Values are based on a 2,000 calorie diet.

Lemony Stuffed Chicken with Bacon

Ingredients

- 8 tbsps olive oil
- 2 tsps lemon juice
- 4 cloves crushed garlic
- 1 tbsp dried oregano
- salt and pepper to taste
- 4 skinless, boneless chicken breasts
- 4 slices feta cheese
- 4 slices bacon, fried and drained

Directions

- Set your oven to 350 degrees before doing anything else.
- Get a bowl, mix: pepper, oils, salt, lemon juice, and garlic.
- Fill your chicken pieces with 1 piece of bacon and 1 piece of feta.

Then stake a toothpick through each.
- Layer your chicken in a casserole dish and coat them with the wet oil mix. Cook everything in the oven for 33 mins.
- Enjoy.

Amount per serving (4 total)

Timing Information:

Preparation	15 m
Cooking	30 m
Total Time	45 m

Nutritional Information:

Calories	483 kcal
Fat	37.1 g
Carbohydrates	3.2g
Protein	33.8 g
Cholesterol	100 mg
Sodium	529 mg

* Percent Daily Values are based on a 2,000 calorie diet.

Baked Chicken Done Right

Ingredients

- 2 tbsps butter
- 1 (4 lb) whole chicken
- salt and pepper to taste
- 1 tsp dried thyme
- 2 carrots, cut in chunks
- paprika to taste
- 8 slices bacon
- 2 C. beef broth

Directions

- Set your oven to 450 degrees before doing anything else.
- Coat your chicken with the following: thyme, butter, paprika, pepper, and salt.
- Fill the chicken with the carrots and then string the legs together.
- Place your bacon on top of the chicken and then run toothpicks

through it to keep the bacon in place.
- Place the chicken in a roasting pan and then pour the broth around the chicken and not on top of it.
- Cook everything for 17 mins in the oven then set the heat to 350 and continue cooking for 80 more mins. Try to baste the chicken at least 4 times while roasting.
- Now take off the bacon from the chicken and baste it one more before cooking in the oven again to get the skin brown and crispy. This should take about 10 to 15 more mins.
- Enjoy.

Amount per serving (6 total)

Timing Information:

Preparation	30 m
Cooking	2 h
Total Time	2 h 30 m

Nutritional Information:

Calories	495 kcal
Fat	32 g
Carbohydrates	2.4g
Protein	46.6 g
Cholesterol	153 mg
Sodium	713 mg

* Percent Daily Values are based on a 2,000 calorie diet.

Buffalo Bacon Sandwich

Ingredients

- 6 slices bacon
- 1/2 C. mayonnaise
- 1/4 C. sour cream
- 2 tbsps hot buffalo wing sauce
- 1 loaf Italian bread, cut in half lengthwise
- 3 C. shredded meat from a rotisserie chicken
- 8 slices pepperjack cheese
- 1/4 C. roasted red bell peppers, drained and sliced (optional)

Directions

- Set your oven to 325 degrees before doing anything else.
- Fry your bacon then place them on some paper towel to drain.
- Get a bowl, mix: hot sauce, mayo, and sour cream.

- Coat your pieces of bread with the mayo mix then layer the chicken, the bacon, and the cheese on one piece.
- Form a sandwich by placing the top portion of the bread over the bottom portion.
- Place a covering of foil around the sandwich and cook everything in the oven for 23 mins.
- Now before serving the sandwich add some pepper slices and cut the sandwich into servings.
- Enjoy.

Amount per serving (8 total)

Timing Information:

Preparation	10 m
Cooking	30 m
Total Time	40 m

Nutritional Information:

Calories	566 kcal
Fat	30.1 g
Carbohydrates	44.3g
Protein	27.9 g
Cholesterol	77 mg
Sodium	988 mg

* Percent Daily Values are based on a 2,000 calorie diet.

Maggie's Easy Fried Rice

Ingredients

- 3 C. water
- 3 C. instant white rice
- 2 tsps vegetable oil
- 3 skinless, boneless chicken breasts, cut into chunks
- 12 slices bacon
- 1 C. chopped green onion
- 1/2 C. soy sauce, or to taste

Directions

- Get your rice boiling in water and cook for 7 mins
- Stir fry your chicken in oil for 9 mins. Then fry then bacon for 4 mins per side in a 2nd pan before breaking the bacon into pieces.
- Add the following to the pan that you fried the bacon in: soy sauce,

rice, green onions, chicken, and bacon.
- Cook the mix for 5 mins.
- Enjoy.

Amount per serving (6 total)

Timing Information:

Preparation	10 m
Cooking	20 m
Total Time	30 m

Nutritional Information:

Calories	384 kcal
Fat	11.5 g
Carbohydrates	42.4g
Protein	25.4 g
Cholesterol	56 mg
Sodium	1668 mg

* Percent Daily Values are based on a 2,000 calorie diet.

Chicken Breast I

(Restaurant Style)

Ingredients

- 6 skinless, boneless chicken breast halves
- 1/4 C. all-purpose flour
- 1/2 tsp salt
- 1 pinch ground black pepper
- 3 tbsps butter
- 1 (14.5 oz.) can stewed tomatoes, with liquid
- 1/2 C. water
- 2 tbsps brown sugar
- 2 tbsps distilled white vinegar
- 2 tbsps Worcestershire sauce
- 1 tsp salt
- 2 tsps chili powder
- 1 tsp mustard powder
- 1/2 tsp celery seed
- 1 clove garlic, minced
- 1/8 tsp hot pepper sauce

Directions

- Get a bowl, mix: black pepper, flour, and half a tsp of salt.
- Coat your chicken with this mix then brown the outsides of the chicken in butter.
- Place your chicken to the side.
- After you have browned all the chicken, in the same pan, add in: hot sauce, tomatoes, garlic, water, celery seed, brown sugar, mustard, vinegar, chili powder, and Worcestershire sauce.
- Get the mix boiling and once it is, add the chicken back in to the sauce.
- Get everything boiling again and then place a lid on the pan, set the heat to low, and let the chicken gently cook for 37 mins, until it is fully done.
- Let the contents cool before serving.
- Enjoy.

Amount per serving (6 total)

Timing Information:

Preparation	30 m
Cooking	40 m
Total Time	1 h 10 m

Nutritional Information:

Calories	247 kcal
Fat	7.8 g
Carbohydrates	14.8g
Protein	28.8 g
Cholesterol	84 mg
Sodium	915 mg

* Percent Daily Values are based on a 2,000 calorie diet.

Chicken Breast II

(Lemon Pepper and Monterey)

Ingredients

- 4 (6 oz.) skinless, boneless chicken breast halves
- 1/4 tsp salt
- 1/4 tsp lemon pepper seasoning
- 1 tbsp vegetable oil
- 8 strips bacon
- 1 onion, sliced
- 1/4 C. packed brown sugar
- 1/2 C. shredded Colby-Monterey Jack cheese

Directions

- Coat your chicken pieces with lemon pepper and salt before stir frying them in oil for 14 mins,

until fully done. Once finished place your chicken to the side.
- Fry your bacon in the same pot for 11 mins and then place them to the side on some paper towels.
- Add in your onions to the bacon fat and stir fry them for 7 mins.
- To serve your chicken wrap each piece with two pieces of bacon and then add a topping of onions and cheese.
- Enjoy.

Amount per serving (4 total)

Timing Information:

Preparation	5 m
Cooking	30 m
Total Time	35 m

Nutritional Information:

Calories	431 kcal
Fat	20.1 g
Carbohydrates	16.9g
Protein	44 g
Cholesterol	124 mg
Sodium	809 mg

* Percent Daily Values are based on a 2,000 calorie diet.

Chicken Breast III

(Stuffed I)

(Sun Dried Tomatoes, Feta, and Spinach)

Ingredients

- 6 skinless, boneless chicken breast halves, flattened
- 1 (8 oz.) bottle Italian-style salad dressing
- 8 slices of stale wheat bread, torn
- 3/4 C. grated Parmesan cheese
- 1 tsp chopped fresh thyme
- 1/8 tsp pepper
- 1 1/2 C. feta cheese, crumbled
- 1/2 C. sour cream
- 1 tbsp vegetable oil
- 3 cloves garlic, minced
- 4 C. chopped fresh spinach
- 1 bunch green onions, chopped
- 1 C. mushrooms, sliced

- 1 (8 oz.) jar oil-packed sun-dried tomatoes, chopped

Directions

- Marinate your chicken in dressing for 1 hr in the fridge.
- Now blend the following: pepper, bread, thyme, and parmesan.
- Make bread crumbs through pulsing the contents multiple times.
- Get a bowl, combine: sour cream and feta.
- Stir fry your garlic and spinach until the spinach is soft then add in the green onions and cook for 4 mins.
- Place the spinach on a plate and then add in your mushrooms and cook everything until it is all tender.
- Add the mushrooms to a plate with the spinach and let it cool.

- Once cool add everything to the feta mix. Then add the sundried tomatoes.
- Pour everything on a baking sheet and then place the sheet in the freezer for 35 mins.
- Now set your oven to 400 degrees before doing anything else.
- Get your chicken pieces and put them in a casserole dish with an equal amount of filling placed on the middle of each.
- Roll up the chicken and stake a toothpick through each one.
- Top with the blended bread and cook everything in oven for 30 mins.
- Enjoy.

Amount per serving (6 total)

Timing Information:

Preparation	1 h
Cooking	45 m
Total Time	2 h 45 m

Nutritional Information:

Calories	633 kcal
Fat	35.9 g
Carbohydrates	34.8g
Protein	44.4 g
Cholesterol	121 mg
Sodium	1555 mg

* Percent Daily Values are based on a 2,000 calorie diet.

Chicken Breast IV

(Pineapple, Brown Sugar, and Onions)

Ingredients

- 10 skinless, boneless chicken breast halves
- 2 C. dry bread crumbs
- 2 tbsps all-purpose flour
- 1 tbsp dried oregano
- 2 tsps salt
- 2 tsps ground black pepper
- 1 tbsp vegetable oil
- 1 1/2 C. packed brown sugar
- 1/4 C. prepared mustard
- 1/2 C. ketchup
- 1 tbsp Worcestershire sauce
- 1 tbsp soy sauce
- 1/4 C. grated onion
- 1/2 tsp salt
- 3/4 C. water
- 10 pineapple rings

Directions

- Clean your chicken under cold water and then add them to a bowl with: pepper, salt (2 tbsps), flour, and bread crumbs.
- Make sure all the chicken pieces are evenly coated.
- Set your oven to 350 degrees before doing anything else.
- For 5 mins on each side fry your chicken, in oil, in a frying pan.
- Then add them to a casserole dish that has been coated with nonstick spray or oil.
- Get a big pot and get the following boiling for 3 mins: water, brown sugar, half a tsp of salt, mustard, onions, ketchup, soy sauce, and Worcestershire.
- Now top your chicken with the boiling mixture and then cook everything in the oven for 60 mins.

- When 5 mins is left in the cooking time put a piece of pineapple on each piece of chicken.
- Enjoy.

Amount per serving (10 total)

Timing Information:

Preparation	15 m
Cooking	1 h
Total Time	1 h 15 m

Nutritional Information:

Calories	425 kcal
Fat	4.4 g
Carbohydrates	65.3g
Protein	31.1 g
Cholesterol	68 mg
Sodium	1142 mg

* Percent Daily Values are based on a 2,000 calorie diet.

Chicken Breast V

(Easy Italian Seasoned)

Ingredients

- 2 large bone-in chicken breast halves with skin
- 1/4 C. extra-virgin olive oil
- 1/2 tsp garlic, minced
- 1/2 tsp coarse sea salt
- 1/2 tsp cracked black pepper
- 1/4 tsp dried rosemary
- 1/4 tsp dried basil

Directions

- Coat your chicken with: basil, olive oil, rosemary, garlic, black pepper, and salt.
- Then place them in a casserole dish and put everything in the fridge for 50 mins.

- Now set your oven to 375 degrees before doing anything else.
- Cook the chicken in the oven for 1 hr.
- Enjoy.

Amount per serving (2 total)

Timing Information:

Preparation	10 m
Cooking	45 m
Total Time	1 h 40 m

Nutritional Information:

Calories	615 kcal
Fat	42.2 g
Carbohydrates	0.7g
Protein	54.5 g
Cholesterol	1153 mg
Sodium	570 mg

* Percent Daily Values are based on a 2,000 calorie diet.

Chicken Breast VI

(Stuffed II)

(Bacon, Garlic, and Feta)

Ingredients

- 1/2 C. mayonnaise
- 1 (10 oz.) package frozen chopped spinach, thawed and drained
- 1/2 C. crumbled feta cheese
- 2 cloves garlic, chopped
- 4 skinless, boneless chicken breasts
- 4 slices bacon

Directions

- Set your oven to 375 degrees before doing anything else.
- Get a bowl, combine: garlic, mayo, feta, and spinach.

- Butterfly your chicken pieces to fill them with an equal amount of mixture. Roll back up your chicken pieces and wrap each one with a piece of bacon before staking each with a toothpick.
- Add your chicken rolls to a casserole dish and place a covering of foil around the dish.
- Cook everything in the oven for 60 mins and check that the internal temp of the chicken is 165 degrees.
- Enjoy.

Amount per serving (4 total)

Timing Information:

Preparation	25 m
Cooking	1 h
Total Time	1 h 25 m

Nutritional Information:

Calories	449 kcal
Fat	32.8 g
Carbohydrates	5.2g
Protein	33.4 g
Cholesterol	104 mg
Sodium	685 mg

* Percent Daily Values are based on a 2,000 calorie diet.

Chicken Breast VII

(Lemon, Dijon, and Rosemary)

Ingredients

- 8 cloves garlic, minced
- 3 tbsps olive oil
- 2 tbsps minced fresh rosemary
- 1 1/2 tbsps Dijon mustard
- 1 1/2 tbsps lemon juice
- 1/4 tsp ground black pepper
- 1/8 tsp kosher salt
- 4 boneless, skinless chicken breast halves

Directions

- Heat up your grill and then coat the grate with some oil.
- Get a bowl, combine: salt, garlic, black pepper, olive oil, lemon juice, rosemary, and mustard.

- Marinate your chicken in this mix for 35 mins, after placing 1/8 of a C. of the marinade to the side for later.
- After the chicken has marinated cook it on the grill for 5 mins then flip it and coat the opposite side with the marinade that was reserved and cook for 6 more mins.
  Cover each piece of chicken with some foil and then let it sit for 5 mins to the side.
- Enjoy.

Amount per serving (4 total)

Timing Information:

Preparation	35 m
Cooking	10 m
Total Time	50 m

Nutritional Information:

Calories	232 kcal
Fat	11.6 g
Carbohydrates	3.9g
Protein	26.7 g
Cholesterol	66 mg
Sodium	276 mg

* Percent Daily Values are based on a 2,000 calorie diet.

Chicken Breast VIII (Easy Flame Broiled)

Ingredients

- 3 tbsps extra virgin olive oil
- 4 bone-in chicken breast halves with skin
- 2 tsps kosher salt
- 1 tsp freshly ground black pepper

Directions

- Turn on your broiler and get it hot, make sure that the rack is at least 6 inches from the source of heat.
- Coat your chicken pieces with pepper, salt, and olive oil and put the skin side downwards on a broiling pan.
- Cook everything in the broiler for 11 mins then turn over the

chicken and cook for 11 more mins.
- Check the internal temp of the chicken. It should be 165 degrees.
- Before serving the chicken let it sit for 10 mins.
- Enjoy.

Amount per serving (4 total)

Timing Information:

Preparation	5 m
Cooking	20 m
Total Time	30 m

Nutritional Information:

Calories	389 kcal
Fat	21.9 g
Carbohydrates	0.3g
Protein	45 g
Cholesterol	127 mg
Sodium	1067 mg

* Percent Daily Values are based on a 2,000 calorie diet.

Chicken Breast IX

(Easy Italian Style)

Ingredients

- 1 1/2 C. shredded Italian cheese blend
- 1 clove garlic, finely chopped
- 1 tsp dried basil
- 1 tsp dried oregano
- 1/2 C. grated Parmesan cheese
- 1/2 C. Italian-seasoned bread crumbs
- 4 boneless, skinless chicken breasts
- 1 egg, well beaten
- 1 C. spaghetti sauce
- 1/4 C. shredded Italian cheese blend, or to taste (optional)

Directions

- Set your oven to 350 degrees before doing anything else.
- Get a bowl, mix: oregano, 1.5 C. of cheese, basil, and garlic.
- Get a 2nd bowl, mix: bread crumbs, and parmesan.
- Butterfly your chicken and then with a mallet flatten it out on a cutting board.
- Divide your mix equally amongst your pieces of chicken placing it in the center of the meat.
- Then the roll up the chicken around the cheese mix and coat the outside with some egg.
- Dip the roll into the parmesan mix and then place everything into a casserole dish that has been coated with nonstick spray.
- Cook the chicken in the oven for 50 mins.
- After the chicken is fully done top it with the pasta sauce and a quarter of a C. of Italian cheese.
- Cook everything for 7 more mins in the oven.

- Enjoy.

Amount per serving (4 total)

Timing Information:

Preparation	20 m
Cooking	50 m
Total Time	1 h 10 m

Nutritional Information:

Calories	470 kcal
Fat	22.7 g
Carbohydrates	21.5g
Protein	43.5 g
Cholesterol	154 mg
Sodium	1008 mg

* Percent Daily Values are based on a 2,000 calorie diet.

Chicken Breast X

(Stuffed III)

(Easy Creole Style)

Ingredients

- 1/2 lb smoked sausage, sliced thinly
- 1/2 lb fresh button mushrooms
- 3 tbsps chopped green onion
- 1 tsp minced garlic
- 4 tbsps blue cheese salad dressing, divided
- 3 skinless, boneless chicken breasts
- 1 tbsp Cajun-style seasoning

Directions

- Stir fry your sausage until browned all over then add in your

mushrooms and continue stirring and frying for 7 mins.
- Now add in: garlic and green onions.
- Cook for 4 more mins.
- Now place this mix in a bowl and process it in a food processor or blender with 1 tbsp of dressing.
- Set your oven to 375 degrees before doing anything else.
- Slice an opening in your chicken and then place an equal amount of mushroom mix in each.
- Coat the chicken pieces with Cajun seasoning and then brown the outsides in a pan, in oil, for about 2 mins each side.
- Once the chicken has been fully browned add everything to a casserole dish and then cover them with the leftover mushroom mix (if any remains), and also any dressing.
- Cook everything in the oven for 35 mins, until the meat is fully done.

- Let the chicken sit for 10 mins before serving.
- Enjoy.

Amount per serving (3 total)

Timing Information:

Preparation	5 m
Cooking	55 m
Total Time	1 h

Nutritional Information:

Calories	553 kcal
Fat	36.5 g
Carbohydrates	7.5g
Protein	47.7 g
Cholesterol	123 mg
Sodium	1914 mg

* Percent Daily Values are based on a 2,000 calorie diet.

Chicken Breast XI

(Cream of Chicken, Stuffing, and Swiss)

Ingredients

- 4 skinless, boneless chicken breast halves
- 8 slices Swiss cheese
- 1 (10.75 oz.) can cream of chicken soup
- 1/2 C. white wine
- 1 C. herb-seasoned stuffing mix, crushed
- 1/4 C. melted butter

Directions

- Set your oven to 350 degrees before doing anything else.
- Get a bowl, combine: wine, soup, and melted butter.

- Layer your chicken in a casserole dish and top with two pieces of cheese, and then the wine mix, and them some stuffing.
- Bake for 60 mins.
- Enjoy.

Amount per serving (4 total)

Timing Information:

Preparation	15 m
Cooking	55 m
Total Time	1 h 10 m

Nutritional Information:

Calories	730 kcal
Fat	36.1 g
Carbohydrates	47.4 g
Protein	46.3 g
Cholesterol	154 mg
Sodium	1543 mg

* Percent Daily Values are based on a 2,000 calorie diet.

Chicken Breast XII

(Onions, Bacon, and Brown Sugar)

Ingredients

- 1/2 C. all-purpose flour
- 1/4 C. seasoned bread crumbs
- 2 tsps garlic salt
- 1 tsp freshly ground black pepper
- 4 (6 oz.) skinless, boneless chicken breast halves, flattened
- 8 bacon strips
- 1 onion, sliced
- 1/4 tsp lemon-pepper seasoning
- 1/4 tsp Italian seasoning
- 1/4 tsp salt
- 1/8 tsp red pepper flakes, or more to taste
- 1/4 C. packed brown sugar
- 1/2 C. shredded Colby-Monterey Jack cheese

Directions

- Get a bowl, combine: black pepper, flour, garlic salt, and bread crumbs.
- Cover your chicken with this mix.
- Fry your bacon for 10 mins then place everything to the side.
- Now stir fry your chicken in the bacon grease for about 7 mins per side until fully done.
- Now place the chicken to the side with the bacon.
- Now turn on your broiler and ensure that the rack is at least 6 inches from the heating source.
- Add to the bacon fat, the following: brown sugar, onions, pepper flakes, lemon pepper, salt, Italian seasoning.
- Stir fry for 13 mins.
- Put your chicken in a broiler pan or cookie sheet and add to 2 pieces of bacon to each and then some onion mix and Monterey.
- Cook everything in the broiler for 2 to 4 mins to melt the cheese.

- Enjoy.

Amount per serving (4 total)

Timing Information:

Preparation	10 m
Cooking	35 m
Total Time	45 m

Nutritional Information:

Calories	664 kcal
Fat	35.7 g
Carbohydrates	34.5g
Protein	48.7 g
Cholesterol	152 mg
Sodium	1823 mg

* Percent Daily Values are based on a 2,000 calorie diet.

Chicken Breast XIII

(Lemon Lime Soda)

Ingredients

- 1 1/2 C. lemon-lime soda
- 1/2 C. olive oil
- 1/2 C. soy sauce
- 1/4 tsp garlic powder
- 4 (6 oz.) skinless, boneless chicken breast halves

Directions

- Get a bowl, combine: garlic powder, lemon soda, soy sauce, and olive oil.
- Combine in your chicken and place in everything the fridge for 8 hrs.
- Now heat up your grill and get the grate coated with oil.

- For 8 mins on each side grill your chicken.
- Let them cool off before serving.
- Enjoy.

Amount per serving (4 total)

Timing Information:

Preparation	5 m
Cooking	15 m
Total Time	8 h 20 m

Nutritional Information:

Calories	488 kcal
Fat	31.6 g
Carbohydrates	12.7g
Protein	37.4 g
Cholesterol	97 mg
Sodium	1899 mg

* Percent Daily Values are based on a 2,000 calorie diet.

Chicken Breast XIV

(Easy Japanese Style)

Ingredients

- 1 lb boneless skinless chicken breasts
- 1 egg
- 1 C. panko crumbs
- 1/2 tsp Sea Salt
- 1/4 tsp Black Pepper
- 1/2 tsp Garlic Powder
- 1/2 tsp Onion Powder
- 1/4 C. Corn Oil

Directions

- With a mallet, flatten your chicken, and then dip them in whisked egg, and a mix of: onion powder, salt, garlic powder, panko, and pepper.

- For 4 mins on each side cook your chicken in hot oil until fully done.
- Drain off excess oils with some paper towel.
- Enjoy.

Amount per serving (4 total)

Timing Information:

Preparation	10 m
Cooking	4 m
Total Time	14 m

Nutritional Information:

Calories	335 kcal
Fat	17.5 g
Carbohydrates	19.6g
Protein	30.8 g
Cholesterol	112 mg
Sodium	546 mg

* Percent Daily Values are based on a 2,000 calorie diet.

Chicken Breast XV

(Tomatoes and Onions)

Ingredients

- 1 (32 fluid oz.) container chicken stock
- 32 fluid oz. water, or more if needed
- 1 yellow onion, peeled and slits cut into it
- 1 bunch celery, stalks (including leaves) separated
- 3 carrots
- 2 tbsps tomato paste, or more to taste
- 1 tbsp salt
- 5 whole black peppercorns
- 1 bay leaf
- 2 lbs skinless, boneless chicken breast halves, each cut in half

Directions

- Get the following boiling: bay leaf, stock, peppercorns, water, salt, onions, tomato paste, carrots, and celery.
- Once everything is boiling set the heat to low and let it gently cook for 40 mins.
- Add in your chicken and make sure ii is fully submerged if not, add some water.
- Get everything boiling again for about 2 mins then add a tight lid on the pot and shut the heat.
- Let the chicken poach for 20 mins until fully done.
- Check the internal temperature of the chicken it should be 165 degrees.
- Enjoy.

Amount per serving (4 total)

Timing Information:

Preparation	15 m
Cooking	45 m
Total Time	1 h

Nutritional Information:

Calories	322 kcal
Fat	3.9 g
Carbohydrates	14.4g
Protein	55.2 g
Cholesterol	1133 mg
Sodium	2786 mg

* Percent Daily Values are based on a 2,000 calorie diet.

Chicken Breast XVI

(Rustic Style)

Ingredients

- 1/4 C. unsalted butter
- 2 bone-in skin-on chicken breasts
- 4 potatoes, peeled and cut into 1-inch cubes
- 4 carrots, peeled and cut into 1/2-inch rounds
- 3 stalks celery, cut into 1/2-inch slices
- 1 tbsp fresh rosemary
- 1 tsp fresh lemon thyme leaves
- 1/2 tsp smoked paprika
- 1/2 tsp garlic powder
- 1/2 tsp seasoned salt
- 1/4 tsp ground white pepper
- salt and ground black pepper to taste

Directions

- Get your thyme and rosemary and chop it nicely then place it to the side in a bowl. Then also add to the spice: black pepper, paprika, salt, garlic powder, white pepper, and season salt.
- Cook your chicken in butter for 6 mins then turn over the chicken and place the following veggies around the chicken: celery, potatoes, and carrots.
- Top everything with the thyme spice mix and put a lid on the pot. Cook for 47 mins with a medium to low level of heat.
- Ensure the internal temp of the chicken is 165 before serving.
- Enjoy.

Amount per serving (4 total)

Timing Information:

Preparation	15 m
Cooking	50 m
Total Time	1 h 5 m

Nutritional Information:

Calories	601 kcal
Fat	23.7 g
Carbohydrates	45.8g
Protein	50.4 g
Cholesterol	1157 mg
Sodium	407 mg

* Percent Daily Values are based on a 2,000 calorie diet.

Chicken Breast XVII (Savory Garlic)

Ingredients

- cooking spray
- 1 clove garlic, minced
- 4 skinless, boneless chicken breast halves
- salt and ground black pepper to taste
- 3/4 C. chicken broth
- 1 tbsp lemon juice

Directions

- Stir fry your garlic, for 5 mins, in a pan with nonstick spray.
- Then add in your chicken after coating it with some pepper and salt and cook for 14 mins.
- Pour in your lemon juice and broth and get everything boiling.

- Once everything is boiling, place a lid on the pot, set the heat to low, and let the chicken gently cook for 17 mins.
- Place your chicken to the side and continue gently cooking your broth mix for about 4 more mins until it has reduced. Then top your chicken with it.
- Enjoy.

Amount per serving (4 total)

Timing Information:

Preparation	10 m
Cooking	25 m
Total Time	35 m

Nutritional Information:

Calories	131 kcal
Fat	2.9 g
Carbohydrates	0.8g
Protein	23.8 g
Cholesterol	66 mg
Sodium	275 mg

* Percent Daily Values are based on a 2,000 calorie diet.

Chicken Breast XVIII

(Teriyaki, Tomatillos, and Muenster)

Ingredients

- 1 (12 fluid oz.) can or bottle beer
- 1/2 C. teriyaki sauce
- 1 tbsp chili powder
- 1 tsp garlic powder
- 8 skinless, boneless chicken breast halves
- 8 slices Muenster cheese
- 3 1/2 lbs fresh tomatillos, husks removed
- 1/2 C. water
- 1 onion, chopped
- 6 cloves garlic, chopped, or more to taste
- 1 pinch salt and ground black pepper to taste
- 1/4 C. chopped fresh cilantro
- 1 C. sour cream

Directions

- Get a bowl, combine: garlic powder, beer, chili powder, and teriyaki. Add in your chicken and place a covering on the bowl, let the chicken marinate overnight.
- Now heat up your grill and get the grate ready by coating it with some oil.
- For 8 mins per side grill your chicken. Then place the cooked chicken in a casserole dish and add a topping of Muenster.
- Now set your oven to 350 degrees before doing anything else.
- Get the following boiling: water and tomatillos.
- Once everything is boiling, place a lid on the pan, set the heat to low, and cook the mix for 11 mins.
- Add in the garlic and onions and also some pepper and salt and gently cook for 17 mins.

- Puree this sauce in a food processor or blender and then once it is smooth add in cilantro and sour cream.
- Blend the mix again and then top your chicken with this sauce.
- Cook everything in the oven for 17 mins.
- Enjoy.

Amount per serving (8 total)

Timing Information:

Preparation	20 m
Cooking	30 m
Total Time	6 h 50 m

Nutritional Information:

Calories	399 kcal
Fat	19.1 g
Carbohydrates	21.8g
Protein	33.4 g
Cholesterol	98 mg
Sodium	948 mg

* Percent Daily Values are based on a 2,000 calorie diet.

Chicken Breast XIX (Dump Dinner Style)

Ingredients

- 1 lb skinless, boneless chicken breast halves
- 1 (14.5 oz.) can petite diced tomatoes
- 1/4 onion, chopped (optional)
- 1 tsp Italian seasoning (optional)
- 1 clove garlic, minced (optional)

Directions

- Add your chicken to a crock pot and then pour in: garlic, tomatoes, Italian seasoning, and onions.
- Let this cook in the slow cooker for 8 hrs. with a low level of heat.
- Let the contents cool for about 10 mins uncovered and then add in

your preferred amount of pepper and salt.
- Enjoy with cooked Jasmin rice.

Amount per serving (4 total)

Timing Information:

Preparation	10 m
Cooking	6 h
Total Time	6 h 10 m

Nutritional Information:

Calories	144 kcal
Fat	2.4 g
Carbohydrates	5.2g
Protein	23.1 g
Cholesterol	59 mg
Sodium	208 mg

* Percent Daily Values are based on a 2,000 calorie diet.

Chicken Breast XX

(Mozzarella, Rosemary, and Marsala)

Ingredients

- 8 skinless, boneless chicken breast halves
- 1/2 C. all-purpose flour
- 1 tsp poultry seasoning
- 1 tbsp butter
- 1 tbsp olive oil
- 1/4 C. Marsala wine
- 1 C. chopped Portobello mushrooms
- 1 C. chopped onion
- 1 tsp dried rosemary
- 4 slices mozzarella cheese

Directions

- Coat your chicken with a mix of poultry seasoning and flour. Then

for 6 mins on each side fry each piece of chicken in butter and then set it to the side.
- Add in your wine and scrape up any browned bits in the pan and then combine in: rosemary, mushrooms, and onions.
- Stir fry everything for 7 mins and then add in your chicken back to the pan.
- Coat your chicken with the sauce and then add a topping of cheese on each.
- Cook the contents for 3 mins with a lid and then shut the heat and let it sit for 12 mins.
- Ensure that your chicken is fully done before serving.
- Enjoy.

Amount per serving (4 total)

Timing Information:

Preparation	10 m
Cooking	50 m
Total Time	1 h

Nutritional Information:

Calories	492 kcal
Fat	13.9 g
Carbohydrates	20.1g
Protein	64 g
Cholesterol	1162 mg
Sodium	352 mg

* Percent Daily Values are based on a 2,000 calorie diet.

Chicken Breast XXI

(Buttery Mushrooms and Cheese)

Ingredients

- 6 skinless, boneless chicken breast halves
- salt and pepper to taste
- 1 pinch paprika, or to taste
- 3 tbsps butter
- 1 (10.75 oz.) can condensed cream of mushroom soup
- 1/3 C. milk
- 2 tbsps minced onion
- 1/2 C. processed cheese (such as Velveeta(R)), diced
- 2 tbsps Worcestershire sauce
- 1 (4.5 oz.) can sliced mushrooms, drained and chopped
- 2/3 C. sour cream

Directions

- Coat a baking dish with oil or nonstick spray and then set your oven to 350 degrees before doing anything else.
- Coat your chicken pieces with: paprika, salt, and pepper and then fry them in butter for 6 mins per side.
- Place all the chicken in the dish.
- Now get a big pot and heat the following but do not boil it: mushrooms, mushroom soup, Worcestershire, milk, cheese, and onions.
- You want to continue heating until everything is hot and the cheese is melted and combined with the mix.
- Top your chicken with this sauce and cook everything in the oven for 46 mins then baste the chicken and cook for 30 more mins.
- Enjoy.

NOTE: If you like you can baste the chicken more than once but at least once is recommended.

Amount per serving (6 total)

Timing Information:

Preparation	25 m
Cooking	1 h 35 m
Total Time	2 h

Nutritional Information:

Calories	335 kcal
Fat	20.6 g
Carbohydrates	8.9g
Protein	28.2 g
Cholesterol	100 mg
Sodium	769 mg

* Percent Daily Values are based on a 2,000 calorie diet.

Chicken Breast XXII

(Bite Sized Bake)

Ingredients

- 1 lb skinless, boneless chicken breast halves - cut into bite size pieces
- 4 tbsps butter, melted
- 1 1/4 C. Italian seasoned bread crumbs

Directions

- Set your oven to 325 degrees before doing anything else.
- Get your margarine melted in a bowl and coat your chicken in it.
- Now dip the coated chicken in breadcrumbs.
- Cook the chicken in the oven for 12 mins then flip them and cook for 8 to 10 more mins.

- Enjoy.

Amount per serving (4 total)

Timing Information:

Preparation	10 m
Cooking	30 m
Total Time	50 m

Nutritional Information:

Calories	371 kcal
Fat	16.3 g
Carbohydrates	25.7g
Protein	29 g
Cholesterol	96 mg
Sodium	798 mg

* Percent Daily Values are based on a 2,000 calorie diet.

Chicken Breast XXIII

(Carrots, Peppers, and Parsley)

Ingredients

- 4 skinless, boneless chicken breast halves
- 8 carrots, sliced into 1/2-inch rounds
- 4 green bell peppers, sliced
- 8 stalks celery, chopped
- 8 green onions, chopped
- 1/4 C. chopped fresh flat-leaf parsley
- 1/2 C. olive oil
- 1 tsp salt
- 1 tsp Italian seasoning
- 1 tsp chili powder
- 1 tsp lemon pepper
- 4 pinches freshly ground black pepper, or to taste

Directions

- Set your oven to 375 degrees before doing anything else.
- Layer your chicken in a casserole dish then surround it with: parsley, carrots, onions, bell peppers, and celery.
- Cover everything with: black and lemon pepper, salt, chili powder, and Italian seasoning.
- Cook the dish in the oven for 35 mins.
- Enjoy.

Amount per serving (4 total)

Timing Information:

Preparation	20 m
Cooking	30 m
Total Time	50 m

Nutritional Information:

Calories	485 kcal
Fat	31.5 g
Carbohydrates	23.8g
Protein	29 g
Cholesterol	69 mg
Sodium	923 mg

* Percent Daily Values are based on a 2,000 calorie diet.

Chicken Breast XXIV

(Pineapple, Lime, and Garlic)

Ingredients

- 1/4 C. olive oil
- 1/4 C. lime juice
- 1 tbsp minced garlic
- 1/2 C. of pineapple, no juice
- salt and ground black pepper to taste
- 2 skinless, boneless chicken breast halves

Directions

- Marinate your chicken in a mix of: black pepper, olive oil, salt, garlic, and lime juice. Let it sit overnight.
- Set your oven to 400 degrees before doing anything else.

- Place your chicken in a casserole dish and then top it with more black pepper and salt before cooking everything in the oven for 35 mins.
- When five mins is left in the cooking time top your chicken with the pineapple chunks.
- Then continue baking.
- Enjoy.

Amount per serving (2 total)

Timing Information:

Preparation	10 m
Cooking	25 m
Total Time	3 h 35 m

Nutritional Information:

Calories	378 kcal
Fat	29.8 g
Carbohydrates	4 g
Protein	24 g
Cholesterol	65 mg
Sodium	58 mg

* Percent Daily Values are based on a 2,000 calorie diet.

Chicken Breast XXV

(Parmesan, Spinach, and Pesto)

Ingredients

- 1 1/2 C. finely chopped fresh spinach
- 2 tbsps basil pesto, or to taste
- 4 skinless, boneless chicken breast halves
- 2 tbsps grated Parmesan cheese (optional)

Directions

- Set your oven to 375 degrees before doing anything else.
- Get a bowl, combine: pesto and spinach.
- Layer half of the mix in a casserole dish then layer your

chicken pieces and top everything with the rest of the mix.
- Place some foil around the casserole dish and cook in the contents in the oven for 35 mins.
- Add your preferred amount of pepper and salt. Then top the chicken with your parmesan.
- Cook everything for 17 more mins in the oven.
- Enjoy.

Amount per serving (4 total)

Timing Information:

Preparation	10 m
Cooking	45 m
Total Time	55 m

Nutritional Information:

Calories	179 kcal
Fat	7.1 g
Carbohydrates	1.3g
Protein	26.5 g
Cholesterol	69 mg
Sodium	169 mg

* Percent Daily Values are based on a 2,000 calorie diet.

Chicken Breast XXVI

(Easy BBQ Style)

(Grilled)

Ingredients

- 2 skinless, boneless chicken breasts
- 1 C. Italian-style salad dressing
- 1 (18 oz.) bottle barbecue sauce

Directions

- Get a bowl and combine in it your frozen chicken and dressing.
- Place a covering over the bowl and then place it in the fridge until the chicken is no longer frozen.
- Now get your grill hot and get the grate ready by coating it with oil.

- For 7 mins per side cook your chicken on the grill.
- Flip the chicken pieces and then coat them with bbq sauce liberally.
- Enjoy.

Amount per serving (2 total)

Timing Information:

Preparation	2 h
Cooking	20 m
Total Time	2 h 30 m

Nutritional Information:

Calories	850 kcal
Fat	35.5 g
Carbohydrates	103.6g
Protein	27.7 g
Cholesterol	68 mg
Sodium	4840 mg

* Percent Daily Values are based on a 2,000 calorie diet.

Chicken Breast XXVII

(Stuffed IV)

(Crawfish, Crab, and Mushrooms)

Ingredients

- 8 skinless, boneless chicken breast halves
- 1 C. Worcestershire sauce
- 2 C. unsalted butter
- 1 C. diced onion
- 1 C. diced celery
- 1/2 C. diced green bell pepper
- 3 tbsps minced garlic
- 1 lb cooked and peeled crawfish tails, coarsely chopped
- salt
- black pepper
- 1 C. all-purpose flour
- 1 pint heavy whipping cream

- 12 oz. fresh oyster mushrooms, stemmed and sliced
- 2 C. fresh lump crabmeat
- 1 C. diced green onion

Directions

- With a mallet flatten your chicken on a working surface then put them in a bowl, with the Worcestershire sauce.
- Place everything in the fridge.
- Meanwhile stir fry your garlic, onions, bell peppers, and celery in butter (half a C.) for 17 mins then combine in the fish and cook for 7 more mins.
- Now add in the pepper and salt.
- Place everything to the side in a big bowl.
- Coat your chicken with some flour and then brown it in butter (half a C.).
- Set your oven to 375 degrees before doing anything else.

- Lay your chicken flat and add an equal amount of crawfish mix to it. Then fold it up and stake a toothpick through it. Place everything in a casserole dish.
- For 7 mins cook the following: green onions, cream, mushrooms, and butter (1 C.).
- Top your chicken wraps with the cream mix and an equal amount of crabmeat.
- Place a wrapping of foil around the entire dish and cook everything in the oven for 50 mins.
- Enjoy.

Amount per serving (8 total)

Timing Information:

Preparation	1 h
Cooking	1 h
Total Time	2 h

Nutritional Information:

Calories	1073 kcal
Fat	72.5 g
Carbohydrates	128.2g
Protein	75.8 g
Cholesterol	1437 mg
Sodium	1715 mg

* Percent Daily Values are based on a 2,000 calorie diet.

Chicken Breast XXVIII

(Coconut Cooked)

(Paleo Approved)

Ingredients

- 3/4 C. coconut milk
- 1 egg
- 6 oz. unsweetened flaked coconut, or more as needed
- 2 lbs skinless, boneless chicken breast halves
- 1/4 C. butter

Directions

- Get a bowl, combine: eggs, and coconut milk.
- Get a 2nd bowl for your coconut flakes.
- With a mallet flatten out your chicken on a working surface.

- Coat the chicken with the egg mix and then the flakes. Layer the chicken in a big dish so as to avoid stacking.
- Fry each piece in butter for 8 mins each side.
- Enjoy.

Amount per serving (4 total)

Timing Information:

Preparation	10 m
Cooking	15 m
Total Time	25 m

Nutritional Information:

Calories	768 kcal
Fat	56.4 g
Carbohydrates	12.1g
Protein	56.3 g
Cholesterol	1215 mg
Sodium	241 mg

* Percent Daily Values are based on a 2,000 calorie diet.

Chicken Breast XXVIII

(Honey Mustard, Savory, and Mushrooms)

Ingredients

- 1/8 C. Italian-style dried bread crumbs
- 4 skinless, boneless chicken breasts
- 1 tbsp olive oil
- 1/2 C. dry white wine
- 1/2 tsp ground savory
- 1/4 tsp salt
- 1 (4.5 oz.) can sliced mushrooms
- 1 tbsp lemon juice
- 1 tbsp honey mustard

Directions

- Coat your chicken pieces with breadcrumbs and then cook each for 4 mins per side.

- Then add in with the chicken: mushrooms, wine, salt, and savory.
- Get the contents boiling, place a lid on the pot, set the heat to low, and gently cook for 17 mins.
- Take out your chicken and place it to the side.
- Add in the mustard and lemon juice to the pot and get it hot for 2 mins.
- Top the chicken with the lemon mix.
- Enjoy.

Amount per serving (4 total)

Timing Information:

Preparation	10 m
Cooking	50 m
Total Time	1 h 20 m

Nutritional Information:

Calories	217 kcal
Fat	5.4 g
Carbohydrates	7.2g
Protein	28.6 g
Cholesterol	69 mg
Sodium	454 mg

* Percent Daily Values are based on a 2,000 calorie diet.

Chicken Breast XXX

(Red Pepper, Cilantro, and Lime)

Ingredients

- 1/2 C. orange juice
- 1/2 lime, juiced
- 1 tbsp honey
- 1 tsp crushed red pepper flakes
- 4 (6 oz.) skinless, boneless chicken breast halves
- 1 tbsp chopped fresh cilantro

Directions

- Get a bowl, combine: pepper flakes, orange juice, honey, and lime juice.
- Place your chicken in the mix and stir everything before placing a covering on the bowl and letting

it marinate in the fridge for 40 mins.
- Get your grill hot and get the grate ready by applying some oil to it.
- Grill the chicken for 7 mins then flip it and cook for 7 more mins.
- Before serving the chicken add a garnishing of cilantro.
- Enjoy.

Amount per serving (4 total)

Timing Information:

Preparation	5 m
Cooking	12 m
Total Time	47 m

Nutritional Information:

Calories	223 kcal
Fat	4.3 g
Carbohydrates	8.9g
Protein	35.8 g
Cholesterol	97 mg
Sodium	86 mg

* Percent Daily Values are based on a 2,000 calorie diet.

Chicken Breast XXXI

(Stuffed V)

(Crab, Cream Cheese, and Garlic)

Ingredients

- 3 oz. cream cheese, softened
- 2 tbsps minced onion
- 2 tbsps chopped fresh parsley
- 1 tsp chopped fresh dill
- 1 tsp minced garlic
- 1/8 tsp lemon pepper
- 4 oz. fresh Dungeness crabmeat
- 4 skinless, boneless chicken breasts
- 1 C. all-purpose flour
- 2 eggs, beaten
- 3 C. fresh bread crumbs
- 2 tbsps butter
- 2 tbsps vegetable oil

Directions

- Get a bowl, mix: lemon pepper, cream cheese, black pepper, crab, garlic, onions, salt, dill, and parsley.
- Place a covering on the bowl, and then enter it into the fridge for 20 mins or until cold.
- Slice an opening into your chicken pieces by cutting a slit through them horizontally.
- Then stuff the chicken pieces with an equal amount of filling. Coat your chicken with whisked egg and then a mix of bread crumbs and flour.
- For 11 mins per side fry the chicken in butter then place them on some paper towel to remove the oil excess.
- Enjoy.

Amount per serving (4 total)

Timing Information:

Preparation	10 m
Cooking	30 m
Total Time	1 h

Nutritional Information:

Calories	569 kcal
Fat	25.4 g
Carbohydrates	41.9g
Protein	42.7 g
Cholesterol	217 mg
Sodium	544 mg

* Percent Daily Values are based on a 2,000 calorie diet.

Chicken Breast XXXII

(Stuffed VI)

(Bacon, Cornbread, and Jam)

Ingredients

- 1 tbsp olive oil
- 2 (6 oz.) skinless, boneless chicken breast halves
- Salt and pepper to taste
- 2 pieces cornbread, crumbled
- 2 slices cooked bacon, crumbled
- 2 tbsps minced celery
- 2 tbsps minced onion
- 2 tbsps butter, melted
- 1/4 C. chicken stock
- 1/3 C. chicken stock
- 1/3 C. plum jam

Directions

- Set your oven to 350 degrees before doing anything else.
- Cut an opening in your chicken pieces before searing them in olive oil. Place them to the side.
- Get a bowl, mix: 1/4 C. chicken stock, cornbread, butter, bacon, onions, and celery. Fill each piece of chicken with this mix.
- Cook the chicken, in a casserole dish, in the oven for 30 mins.
- At the same time get 1/3 a C. of stock boiling then add in jam and gently cook with a low heat until the stock has cooked out.
- Halfway through the cooking time of the chicken, top it with the plum sauce and continue cooking in the oven.
- Enjoy.

Amount per serving (2 total)

Timing Information:

Preparation	15 m
Cooking	40 m
Total Time	55 m

Nutritional Information:

Calories	684 kcal
Fat	30 g
Carbohydrates	61.1g
Protein	42.1 g
Cholesterol	156 mg
Sodium	867 mg

* Percent Daily Values are based on a 2,000 calorie diet.

Chicken Breast XXXIII

(Tarragon, Olives, and Lemon)

Ingredients

- 2 tbsps butter
- 2 tbsps minced garlic
- 1 large lemon, juiced
- 1/2 tsp dried tarragon
- 4 boneless, skinless chicken breasts
- 20 pitted green olives

Directions

- Set your oven to 350 degrees before doing anything else.
- Stir fry: tarragon, garlic, and lemon juice in butter for 1 min.
- Then add in your chicken and cook for 6 mins each side.

- Pour in the olives and cook for 1 more min before entering the pan into the oven for 25 mins.
- Enjoy.

Amount per serving (4 total)

Timing Information:

Preparation	10 m
Cooking	30 m
Total Time	40 m

Nutritional Information:

Calories	216 kcal
Fat	11.2 g
Carbohydrates	4.7g
Protein	25.5 g
Cholesterol	82 mg
Sodium	569 mg

* Percent Daily Values are based on a 2,000 calorie diet.

Chicken Breast XXXIV

(Stuffed VII)

(Peppers, Onions, Squash, and Cheddar)

Ingredients

- 1 tbsp butter
- 1/2 C. finely diced acorn squash
- 1 green bell pepper, diced
- 1 small onion, finely diced
- 1 stalk celery, chopped
- salt and pepper to taste
- 4 skinless, boneless chicken breasts
- 2 oz. shredded Cheddar cheese
- 2 C. all-purpose flour for coating

Directions

- Coat a casserole dish with nonstick spray or oil and then set

your oven to 350 degrees before doing anything else.
- Stir fry your celery, squash, onions, and bell peppers in butter until soft then add in some pepper and salt.
- Shut the heat and add in the cheese.
- Stir the mix a bit.
- Cut an opening into your chicken pieces and add an equal amount of mix to each. Coat the chicken with flour and sear it in a pan with some oil.
- After searing the chicken pieces.
- Layer them in the casserole dish and cook for 35 mins in the oven.
- Enjoy.

Amount per serving (4 total)

Timing Information:

Preparation	10 m
Cooking	1 h
Total Time	1 h 20 m

Nutritional Information:

Calories	461 kcal
Fat	9.8 g
Carbohydrates	53g
Protein	37.9 g
Cholesterol	91 mg
Sodium	197 mg

* Percent Daily Values are based on a 2,000 calorie diet.

Chicken Breast XXXV

(Easy Artisan Style)

Ingredients

- 1 tbsp olive oil
- 3 skinless, boneless chicken breast halves
- 1 tbsp ground black pepper, or to taste
- 3 tbsps onion powder, or to taste
- 1 (28 oz.) can chopped stewed tomatoes, 1/2 the liquid reserved
- 1 (14 oz.) can chicken broth
- 1 (10 oz.) package frozen mixed vegetables
- 1/4 C. water

Directions

- Coat your chicken with some onion power and pepper before cooking for 3 mins per side in oil.

- Add in the tomatoes with juice and the broth.
- Get everything boiling, then place a lid on the pot, set the heat to low, and let the contents cook for 17 mins on each side.
- At the same time get your veggies boiling in water.
- Once everything is boiling add about 3/4 of a C. of tomato mix to the veggies and cook for 7 more mins.
- Remove all the liquid and then serve the veggies with chicken on top.
- Liberally top the chicken and veggies with more tomato sauce.
- Enjoy.

Amount per serving (3 total)

Timing Information:

Preparation	10 m
Cooking	35 m
Total Time	45 m

Nutritional Information:

Calories	325 kcal
Fat	8.3 g
Carbohydrates	36.2g
Protein	30 g
Cholesterol	64 mg
Sodium	1302 mg

* Percent Daily Values are based on a 2,000 calorie diet.

Chicken Breast XXXVI

(Nutmeg, Almonds, and Mushrooms)

Ingredients

- 4 skinless, boneless chicken breast halves
- salt and pepper to taste
- 1 egg
- 1/2 C. water
- 2 C. finely chopped almonds
- 1/4 C. butter
- 3 tbsps olive oil
- 1 lb fresh mushrooms
- 1 onion, sliced into rings
- 2 cloves garlic, crushed
- 1 C. heavy cream
- 1/4 C. almond paste
- 1/2 tsp freshly ground nutmeg

Directions

- With a mallet flatten your chicken and then top everything with some pepper and salt.
- Now set your oven to 350 degrees before doing anything else.
- Get a bowl, and combine in: water and eggs.
- Get a 2nd bowl for the almond crumbs.
- Dip your chicken in the eggs first and then crumbs then sear each piece in butter.
- Place everything in a casserole dish.
- Stir fry your onions, garlic, and mushrooms for 5 mins then top your chicken with it.
- In the same pan combine the almond paste and cream and get it hot but not boiling then add the nutmeg and then pour it over the chicken as well.
- Cook everything in the oven for 45 mins.
- Enjoy.

Amount per serving (4 total)

Timing Information:

Preparation	20 m
Cooking	40 m
Total Time	1 h

Nutritional Information:

Calories	1095 kcal
Fat	88.8 g
Carbohydrates	133.1g
Protein	52.1 g
Cholesterol	1227 mg
Sodium	206 mg

* Percent Daily Values are based on a 2,000 calorie diet.

Chicken Breast XXXVII

(Sweet Potatoes and Balsamic)

Ingredients

- 2 sweet potatoes, peeled and cut into 2-inch pieces
- 1 tbsp olive oil
- salt and pepper to taste
- 2 skinless, boneless chicken breast halves
- 1/2 C. balsamic vinegar
- salt and ground black pepper to taste
- 1/2 C. balsamic vinegar

Directions

- Set your oven to 400 degrees before doing anything else.
- Get a bowl, combine: potatoes, olive oil, pepper and salt.

- Once everything is evenly coated place them in a baking dish and cook everything in the oven for 30 mins.
- Coat your chicken with pepper and salt and then layer them in another casserole dish. Top the chicken with half a C. of balsamic.
- Wrap foil around the dish and cook everything in the oven for 20 mins.
- Turn your potatoes and chicken over and then cook for 20 more mins with a 350 degree level of heat.
- Meanwhile boil the remaining balsamic (half a C.) until half of it has evaporated.
- When the chicken and potatoes are done top them with the balsamic before serving.
- Enjoy.

Amount per serving (2 total)

Timing Information:

Preparation	10 m
Cooking	50 m
Total Time	1 h

Nutritional Information:

Calories	379 kcal
Fat	8.5 g
Carbohydrates	44.7g
Protein	29.8 g
Cholesterol	68 mg
Sodium	179 mg

* Percent Daily Values are based on a 2,000 calorie diet.

Chicken Breast XXXVIII

(Creamy Raspberries and Shallots)

Ingredients

- 2 skinless, boneless chicken breasts
- 2 tbsps butter
- 1 tbsp vegetable oil
- 3 tbsps shallots, minced
- 1/3 C. chicken stock
- 1/4 C. raspberry vinegar
- 1/3 C. heavy whipping cream
- salt and pepper to taste

Directions

- Fry your chicken in a big pot in butter until fully done then place them to the side.
- In the same pan add: chicken stock, and shallots.

- Cook for 5 mins then add the vinegar and get everything boiling.
- Boil and stir until you find that the stock has become a bit thicker and then add the cream and the chicken.
- Cook for 3 mins then add some pepper and salt.
- Enjoy.

Amount per serving (4 total)

Timing Information:

Preparation	10 m
Cooking	30 m
Total Time	1 h

Nutritional Information:

Calories	229 kcal
Fat	17.3 g
Carbohydrates	4 g
Protein	14.3 g
Cholesterol	77 mg
Sodium	91 mg

* Percent Daily Values are based on a 2,000 calorie diet.

Chicken Breast XXXIX

(Lime and Chives)

Ingredients

- 4 skinless, boneless chicken breast halves - flattened
- 1 egg, beaten
- 2/3 C. dry bread crumbs
- 2 tbsps olive oil
- 1 lime, juiced
- 6 tbsps butter
- 1 tsp minced fresh chives
- 1/2 tsp dried dill weed

Directions

- Get a bowl for your eggs.
- Get a 2nd bowl for your bread crumbs.
- Dip your chicken pieces first in eggs and then in the crumbs.

- Now place them on a wire rack, in the open, for 15 mins, to dry out.
- For 6 mins on each side fry your chicken in olive oil then place them to the side.
- Remove any excess oils then add the butter and lime juice.
- Heat and stir for a few mins until the butter is fully melted than add the dill and chives.
- Top the chicken with the lime juice and serve.
- Enjoy.

Amount per serving (4 total)

Timing Information:

Preparation	15 m
Cooking	15 m
Total Time	30 m

Nutritional Information:

Calories	455 kcal
Fat	30 g
Carbohydrates	15.3g
Protein	30.7 g
Cholesterol	164 mg
Sodium	335 mg

* Percent Daily Values are based on a 2,000 calorie diet.

Chicken Breast XL

(Maple Syrup and Pecans)

Ingredients

- 4 skinless, boneless chicken breasts
- 2 tbsps real maple syrup
- 1 C. chopped pecans
- 3 tbsps all-purpose flour
- 1 tsp salt
- 2 tbsps butter
- 1 tbsp vegetable oil

Directions

- Get a bowl, combine: salt, flour, and pecans.
- Coat your chicken pieces with syrup then cover each piece with the pecans.
- Fry these chicken pieces in butter for 14 mins.

- Enjoy with some cooked brown rice.

Amount per serving (4 total)

Timing Information:

Preparation	10 m
Cooking	15 m
Total Time	25 m

Nutritional Information:

Calories	447 kcal
Fat	30.3 g
Carbohydrates	15g
Protein	30.4 g
Cholesterol	84 mg
Sodium	700 mg

* Percent Daily Values are based on a 2,000 calorie diet.

Chicken Breast XLI

(Easy Backroad Style)

Ingredients

- 4 skinless, boneless chicken breast halves
- 1 C. Worcestershire sauce
- 1 C. vegetable oil
- 1 C. lemon juice
- 1 tsp garlic powder

Directions

- Get a bowl, combine: garlic, Worcestershire, lemon juice, and oil. Place a lid on the bowl, and marinate everything in the fridge overnight.
- Turn on your oven's broiler and ensure that the grate is 6 inches away from the heating source.

- Once the broiler is hot, broil your chicken for 8 mins per side until cooked fully.
- Enjoy.

Amount per serving (4 total)

Timing Information:

Preparation	10 m
Cooking	20 m
Total Time	8 h 30 m

Nutritional Information:

Calories	676 kcal
Fat	57.4 g
Carbohydrates	19g
Protein	23.3 g
Cholesterol	61 mg
Sodium	717 mg

* Percent Daily Values are based on a 2,000 calorie diet.

Chicken Breast XLII

(Stuffed VIII)

(Apples and Cheddar)

Ingredients

- 2 skinless, boneless chicken breasts
- 1/2 C. chopped apple
- 2 tbsps shredded Cheddar cheese
- 1 tbsp Italian-style dried bread crumbs
- 1 tbsp butter
- 1/4 C. dry white wine
- 1/4 C. water
- 1 tbsp water
- 1 1/2 tsps cornstarch
- 1 tbsp chopped fresh parsley, for garnish

Directions

- Get a bowl, mix: bread crumbs, cheese, and apples.
- With a mallet pound out your chicken pieces, then add an equal amount of filling to the center of each.
- Shape the chicken pieces into a roll and then stake a toothpick through each.
- Sear your chicken in butter then once it is browned all over add your water and wine.
- Place a lid on the pan and let the contents gently cook for 17 mins.
- Place your chicken on a serving platter and then add some cornstarch and a tbsp of water to the remaining wine in the pot.
- Heat and stir the cornstarch to form a gravy to top your chicken with.
- Serve the chicken rolls with a topping of parsley and gravy.
- Enjoy.

Amount per serving (4 total)

Timing Information:

Preparation	15 m
Cooking	25 m
Total Time	40 m

Nutritional Information:

Calories	139 kcal
Fat	5.1 g
Carbohydrates	4.9g
Protein	15 g
Cholesterol	46 mg
Sodium	120 mg

* Percent Daily Values are based on a 2,000 calorie diet.

Chicken Breast XLIII

(Buttery Capers and Lemon)

Ingredients

- 4 boneless, skinless chicken breast halves
- 1 tsp lemon pepper
- 1 tsp salt
- 1 tsp dried dill weed
- 1 tsp garlic powder
- 3 tbsps butter
- 1/2 C. whipping cream
- 2 tbsps capers, drained and rinsed

Directions

- Coat your chicken with garlic powder, lemon pepper, dill, and salt. Then for 6 mins sear the chicken in butter making sure to turn the chicken repeatedly.

- Set your heat to low and cook the contents for 8 mins until fully done.
- Place your chicken to the side and wrap them with some foil.
- In the same pan turn up the heat and add in whipping cream.
- Cook the cream for 4 mins while stirring then add the capers.
- Top the chicken with the cream and serve with some cooked angel hair pasta.
- Enjoy.

Amount per serving (4 total)

Timing Information:

Preparation	5 m
Cooking	15 m
Total Time	20 m

Nutritional Information:

Calories	313 kcal
Fat	21.2 g
Carbohydrates	1.8g
Protein	28.2 g
Cholesterol	132 mg
Sodium	974 mg

* Percent Daily Values are based on a 2,000 calorie diet.

Chicken Breast XLIV

(Buttermilk and Honey)

Ingredients

- 3 C. cold water
- 1/4 C. kosher salt
- 1/4 C. honey
- 4 boneless skinless chicken breast halves
- 1/4 C. buttermilk
- 1 C. all-purpose flour
- 1 tsp black pepper
- 1/2 tsp garlic salt
- 1/2 tsp onion salt
- cayenne pepper to taste
- vegetable oil for frying

Directions

- Get a bowl, combine: honey, water, and salt.

- Stir the mix for a few mins then add in your chicken and place everything in the fridge for 60 mins covered.
- Then drain the liquid.
- Add in your buttermilk and let the chicken sit in the milk for 20 mins.
- Get a 2nd bowl, add: cayenne, flour, onion salt, black pepper, and garlic salt.
- Dredge the chicken in the flour and then place them in on a wire rack for 20 mins.
- Get your veggie oil hot then fry the chicken in it for 16 mins. Ensure that the internal temperature of the chicken is 165 before serving.
- Let the chicken cool for 10 mins.
- Enjoy.

Amount per serving (4 total)

Timing Information:

Preparation	10 m
Cooking	15 m
Total Time	1 h 45 m

Nutritional Information:

Calories	481 kcal
Fat	21.5 g
Carbohydrates	49.4g
Protein	22.8 g
Cholesterol	65 mg
Sodium	6378 mg

* Percent Daily Values are based on a 2,000 calorie diet.

Chicken Breast XLV

(Chili I)

Ingredients

- 1 tsp vegetable oil
- 2 boneless, skinless chicken breast halves
- 1 tsp vegetable oil
- 1 large onion, diced
- salt and freshly ground black pepper to taste
- 4 cloves garlic, chopped
- 1 tbsp ancho chile powder
- 1 tsp ground cumin
- 1 tsp all-purpose flour
- 1/2 tsp chipotle pepper powder
- 1/4 tsp dried oregano
- 1 tsp fine cornmeal
- 2 C. chicken broth, divided
- 2 (15 oz.) cans white beans, drained
- 1 C. chicken broth
- 1/4 tsp white sugar, or to taste

- 1 pinch cayenne pepper, or to taste
- 1/3 C. chopped green onions
- 1/3 C. sour cream
- 1/3 C. chopped fresh cilantro

Directions

- Sear your chicken in veggie oil (1 tsp) for 5 mins then lower the heat and turn over the chicken.
- Cook for 1 more min before placing a lid on the pot and cooking for 4 more mins.
- Ensure the chicken is fully done then cube the chicken after it has cooled off.
- Add in another tsp of oil to the pot and stir fry your onions for 7 mins then add some pepper and salt.
- Combine in the garlic and cook for 2 more mins.
- Now add: oregano, chili powder, chipotle powder, cumin, and flour.

- Cook for 3 mins then add the 1 C. of broth and scrape the browned bits in the bottom of the pan.
- Add the cornmeal and get it boiling.
- Once everything is boiling add the beans and another C. of broth.
- Lower the heat and gently cook the contents.
- Now add the chicken back in along with: cayenne, another C. of broth, sugar, salt, and black pepper.
- Heat everything up and then shut the heat.
- Let the content sit for about 2 mins.
- When serving, add a topping of cilantro, onions, and a dollop of sour cream.
- Enjoy.

Amount per serving (4 total)

Timing Information:

Preparation	20 m
Cooking	30 m
Total Time	50 m

Nutritional Information:

Calories	410 kcal
Fat	8.9 g
Carbohydrates	54.7g
Protein	29.1 g
Cholesterol	41 mg
Sodium	772 mg

* Percent Daily Values are based on a 2,000 calorie diet.

Chicken Breast XLVI (Restaurant Style II)

Ingredients

- 2 large skinless, boneless chicken breast halves
- salt and black pepper to taste
- 8 asparagus spears, trimmed - divided
- 1/2 C. shredded mozzarella cheese, divided
- 1/4 C. Italian seasoned bread crumbs

Directions

- Coat a casserole dish with oil or nonstick spray and then set your oven to 375 degrees before doing anything else.
- With a mallet pound out your chicken breast on a working

surface then top everything with pepper and salt.
- Put 4 pieces of asparagus in the middle of each, then a quarter of a C. of cheese.
- Shape the chicken into rolls then layer them in the casserole dish with the seam portion facing downwards.
- Top each one with 2 tbsps of bread crumbs.
- Cook everything in the oven for 30 mins.
- Enjoy.

Amount per serving (2 total)

Timing Information:

Preparation	20 m
Cooking	25 m
Total Time	45 m

Nutritional Information:

Calories	390 kcal
Fat	10.8 g
Carbohydrates	13.3g
Protein	57.4 g
Cholesterol	1147 mg
Sodium	581 mg

* Percent Daily Values are based on a 2,000 calorie diet.

Chicken Breast XLVII

(Artisan Style II with Artichokes)

Ingredients

- 1 C. whole wheat or white flour
- 1/2 tsp salt
- 1/8 tsp white pepper, or to taste
- 1/8 tsp black pepper, or to taste
- 2 lbs chicken breast tenderloins or strips
- 2 tbsps canola oil
- 2 tbsps extra-virgin olive oil
- 2 C. chicken broth
- 2 tbsps fresh lemon juice
- 1 (12 oz.) jar quartered marinated artichoke hearts, with liquid
- 1/4 C. capers
- 2 tbsps butter
- 1/4 C. chopped flat-leaf parsley

Directions

- Get a bowl, mix: black pepper, flour, white pepper, and salt.
- Coat your chicken with the flour mix then fry them in olive and canola oil until fully done. Then place to the side.
- Now pour in lemon juice and broth then get it simmering and then add in the capers and artichokes.
- Get it simmering again.
- Continue to simmer with a low level of heat until half of the liquid has evaporated.
- Add the butter into the mix and let it melt before adding back in the chicken and simmering for 3 mins.
- Serve the chicken with some parsley and a liberal amount of sauce.
- Enjoy.

Amount per serving (6 total)

Timing Information:

Preparation	20 m
Cooking	20 m
Total Time	40 m

Nutritional Information:

Calories	408 kcal
Fat	18.6 g
Carbohydrates	22g
Protein	40.1 g
Cholesterol	98 mg
Sodium	719 mg

* Percent Daily Values are based on a 2,000 calorie diet.

Chicken Breast XLVIII

(Stuffed IX)

(Honey Mustard, Brown Mustard, and Ham)

Ingredients

- 4 skinless, boneless chicken breast halves
- 4 slices deli ham
- 3/4 C. shredded mozzarella cheese
- 3/4 C. honey
- 1/4 C. spicy brown mustard
- 1/4 C. yellow mustard

Directions

- Coat a casserole dish with nonstick spray and then set your oven to 375 degrees before doing anything else.

- With a mallet flatten your pieces of chicken then place a piece of ham and an equal amount of cheese on each.
- Now roll up the chicken and stake a toothpick through it.
- Layer the chicken pieces in the casserole dish.
- Get a bowl, combine: yellow mustard, honey, and brown mustard.
- Top the chicken with this mix and place a wrapping of foil around the dish as well.
- Cook everything in the oven for 45 mins.
- Enjoy.

Amount per serving (4 total)

Timing Information:

Preparation	15 m
Cooking	40 m
Total Time	55 m

Nutritional Information:

Calories	471 kcal
Fat	13 g
Carbohydrates	54.6g
Protein	36.6 g
Cholesterol	97 mg
Sodium	928 mg

* Percent Daily Values are based on a 2,000 calorie diet.

Chicken Breast XLIX

(Chili II)

Ingredients

- 1/2 C. shredded Cheddar cheese
- 1/4 C. chopped green bell pepper
- 1/4 C. chopped red bell pepper
- 1/4 C. minced cilantro
- 1/4 C. diced tomatoes
- 1/2 tsp chili powder
- 1/2 tsp ground cumin
- 1/8 tsp salt
- 4 skinless, boneless chicken breast halves - flattened
- toothpicks

Directions

- Get a bowl, combine: salt, tomatoes, cumin, cheddar, chili powder, cilantro, red and green peppers.

- Dip your chicken breasts in the mix and then roll them up.
- Place a toothpick in each piece of chicken and put the rolls in the slow cooker.
- Add the rest of the mix to the slow cooker and then cook everything for 90 mins with high heat.
- Enjoy.

Amount per serving (4 total)

Timing Information:

Preparation	20 m
Cooking	3 h
Total Time	3 h 20 m

Nutritional Information:

Calories	199 kcal
Fat	8.3 g
Carbohydrates	2.1g
Protein	27.6 g
Cholesterol	79 mg
Sodium	259 mg

* Percent Daily Values are based on a 2,000 calorie diet.

Chicken Breast L

(Goat Cheese and Balsamic)

Ingredients

- 1 tsp olive oil
- 1 shallot, finely diced
- 1 C. balsamic vinegar
- 2 skinless, boneless chicken breast halves
- 2 oz. goat cheese, divided

Directions

- Set your oven to 350 degrees before doing anything else.
- Stir fry your shallots in olive oil for 7 mins then add in the balsamic and cook for 12 mins while stirring with a low heat and a gentle boil.
- With a mallet flatten your chicken pieces then add: half of the

cheese, and 1/3 of the balsamic mix.
- Roll up the chicken pieces around the mix and then stake a toothpick through each before layering them all in a casserole dish.
- Pour the rest of the balsamic over the chicken in the dish and then cook everything in the oven for 40 mins.
- Enjoy.

Amount per serving (2 total)

Timing Information:

Preparation	15 m
Cooking	30 m
Total Time	45 m

Nutritional Information:

Calories	340 kcal
Fat	13.5 g
Carbohydrates	23.5g
Protein	30.1 g
Cholesterol	83 mg
Sodium	230 mg

* Percent Daily Values are based on a 2,000 calorie diet.

Chicken Thighs I

(Mandarin Chicken)

Ingredients

- 1 C. orange juice
- 1 tbsp soy sauce
- 1 (1 oz.) envelope dry onion soup mix
- 1/2 tsp garlic powder, or to taste
- 8 chicken thighs

Directions

- Set your oven to 350 degrees before doing anything else.
- Get a bowl, combine: garlic powder, orange juice, onion soup, and soy sauce.
- Clean your chicken under fresh cold water then enter them into a casserole dish.

- Top the chicken pieces with the onion soup mix.
- Now cook everything in the oven for 90 mins.
- Baste the chicken every 20 mins.
- Enjoy.

Amount per serving (8 total)

Timing Information:

Preparation	5 m
Cooking	1 h 30 m
Total Time	1 h 35 m

Nutritional Information:

Calories	180 kcal
Fat	9.9 g
Carbohydrates	5.7g
Protein	16.4 g
Cholesterol	59 mg
Sodium	475 mg

* Percent Daily Values are based on a 2,000 calorie diet.

Chicken Thighs II

(Honey and Sriracha)

Ingredients

- 1/2 C. rice vinegar
- 5 tbsps honey
- 1/3 C. soy sauce (such as Silver Swan(R))
- 1/4 C. Asian (toasted) sesame oil
- 3 tbsps Sriracha
- 3 tbsps minced garlic
- salt to taste
- 8 skinless, boneless chicken thighs
- 1 tbsp chopped green onion (optional)

Directions

- Get a bowl, combine: salt, vinegar, garlic, honey, sriracha, soy sauce, and sesame oil.

- Divide the sauce amongst two bowls.
- Put your chicken pieces into one of the bowls, then evenly coat them with sauce, and place them in the fridge, with a covering of plastic, for 60 mins.
- Set your oven to 425 degrees before doing anything else.
- Now a get a pan and boil the remaining half of the marinade for 4 mins while stirring.
- Now put your chicken in a casserole dish and top with one third of the sauce in the pan.
- Cook everything in the oven for 35 mins and baste every 10 mins.
- Let the chicken sit for 15 mins while you get your sauce heated again. Once it is hot again top the chicken with the rest of the hot sauce.
- Enjoy.

Amount per serving (4 total)

Timing Information:

Preparation	5 m
Cooking	30 m
Total Time	1 h 40 m

Nutritional Information:

Calories	544 kcal
Fat	30.2 g
Carbohydrates	26.6g
Protein	40.6 g
Cholesterol	142 mg
Sodium	1814 mg

* Percent Daily Values are based on a 2,000 calorie diet.

Chicken Thighs III

(Syrup and Sriracha)

Ingredients

- 1 clove garlic, sliced, or more to taste
- 2 tsps Asian chili pepper sauce, sriracha
- 1 1/2 tbsps maple syrup
- 2 tbsps soy sauce
- 2 tbsps mayonnaise
- 3 tbsps rice vinegar
- salt and freshly ground black pepper to taste
- 2 lbs skinless, boneless chicken thighs
- 1 lime, cut into 8 wedges

Directions

- Place your garlic in a bowl and mash it until pasty.

- Then add in: vinegar, chili pepper sauce, mayo, syrup, and soy sauce.
- Place your chicken thighs in a casserole dish and top them with the garlic sauce.
- Place some plastic around the dish and chill everything it in the fridge for 3 hours.
- Then add some salt to it.
- Grill your chicken pieces for 4 mins per side.
- Then continue cooking for about 8 more mins flipping the chicken every 2 or 3 mins.
- Garnish your chicken with lime wedges.
- Enjoy.

Amount per serving (8 total)

Timing Information:

Preparation	15 m
Cooking	20 m
Total Time	3 h 40 m

Nutritional Information:

Calories	194 kcal
Fat	10.8 g
Carbohydrates	4g
Protein	19.5 g
Cholesterol	71 mg
Sodium	311 mg

* Percent Daily Values are based on a 2,000 calorie diet.

Chicken Thighs IV

(Creamy Mushrooms and Onions)

Ingredients

- 8 chicken thighs
- 1 tbsp vegetable oil
- 1 pinch ground black pepper
- 1 pinch salt
- 1 pinch paprika
- 1 (10.75 oz.) can condensed cream of mushroom soup
- 1 (1 oz.) package dry onion soup mix
- 1 C. sour cream
- 1 tbsp lemon juice
- 1 tsp dried dill weed

Directions

- Get a frying and pan and with some hot oil brown the chicken all over.
- Then add everything to a casserole dish and top with paprika, pepper, and salt.
- Get a bowl, combine: dill, mushroom soup, lemon juice, onion soup, and sour cream.
- Combine everything until smooth and evenly top your chicken with this mix.
- Cook the contents in the oven for 60 mins.
- Enjoy.

Amount per serving (4 total)

Timing Information:

Preparation	10 m
Cooking	1 h
Total Time	1 h 20 m

Nutritional Information:

Calories	637 kcal
Fat	48.8 g
Carbohydrates	12.7g
Protein	36.1 g
Cholesterol	183 mg
Sodium	1284 mg

* Percent Daily Values are based on a 2,000 calorie diet.

Chicken Thighs V

(French Style and Apricots)

Ingredients

- 12 chicken thighs
- 1 C. apricot preserves
- 1 C. French dressing
- 1 (1 oz.) package dry onion soup mix

Directions

- Set your oven to 350 degrees before doing anything else.
- Get a bowl, combine: soup, apricots, and dressing.
- Get a casserole dish and place your chicken in it then top with the apricot mix.
- Cook everything in the oven for 1 hr.
- Enjoy.

Amount per serving (12 total)

Timing Information:

Preparation	10 m
Cooking	1 h
Total Time	1 h 20 m

Nutritional Information:

Calories	342 kcal
Fat	20.1 g
Carbohydrates	23.3g
Protein	15.9 g
Cholesterol	59 mg
Sodium	444 mg

* Percent Daily Values are based on a 2,000 calorie diet.

Chicken Thighs VI

(Dijon, Brown Sugar, and Cayenne)

Ingredients

- 8 large bone-in, skin-on chicken thighs
- 1/2 C. Dijon mustard
- 1/4 C. packed brown sugar
- 1/4 C. red wine vinegar
- 1 tsp dry mustard powder
- 1 tsp salt
- 1 tsp freshly ground black pepper
- 1/2 tsp ground dried chipotle pepper
- 1 pinch cayenne pepper, or to taste
- 4 cloves garlic, minced
- 1 onion, sliced into rings
- 2 tsps vegetable oil, or as needed

Directions

- Get a bowl, combine: cayenne, Dijon, chipotle, vinegar, black pepper, mustard powder, and salt.
- Take your chicken and cut some incisions in them (at least 2). Then place everything in the bowl.
- Place a covering of plastic around the bowl, and put everything in the fridge for 5 to 8 hrs.
- Cover a casserole dish with foil and then set your oven to 450 degrees before doing anything else.
- Pour your onions around the dish and then layer the chicken on top.
- Coat everything with some veggies and top the contents with some cayenne and salt.
- Cook everything in the oven for 50 mins.
- Then plate the chicken.
- Now boil the drippings for 5 mins while stirring.

- Finally top the chicken and onions with the sauce.
- Enjoy.

Amount per serving (8 total)

Timing Information:

Preparation	20 m
Cooking	40 m
Total Time	5 h

Nutritional Information:

Calories	352 kcal
Fat	19 g
Carbohydrates	13.8g
Protein	29.1 g
Cholesterol	106 mg
Sodium	765 mg

* Percent Daily Values are based on a 2,000 calorie diet.

Chicken Thighs VII

(Onions, Carrots, and Rosemary)

Ingredients

- 6 chicken thighs
- salt and ground black pepper to taste
- 1 yellow onion, diced
- 1/4 C. chopped fresh basil, or to taste
- 3 cloves garlic, sliced
- 2 tsps finely chopped fresh rosemary
- 1 1/2 C. chicken broth
- 3 C. diced carrots

Directions

- Set your oven to 375 degrees before doing anything else.

- Place your chicken in a casserole dish and then top everything with: rosemary, basil, garlic, carrots, pepper, salt, and onions.
- Now cover everything in the broth.
- Wrap some foil around the top of the casserole dish and cook the contents in the oven for 65 mins.
- After 65 mins has elapsed remove the covering on the dish and continue cooking for 10 more mins.
- Enjoy.

Amount per serving (6 total)

Timing Information:

Preparation	15 m
Cooking	1 h 10 m
Total Time	1 h 25 m

Nutritional Information:

Calories	238 kcal
Fat	12.2 g
Carbohydrates	10.8g
Protein	20.6 g
Cholesterol	72 mg
Sodium	352 mg

* Percent Daily Values are based on a 2,000 calorie diet.

Chicken Thighs VIII

(American Style I)

Ingredients

- cooking spray
- 8 bone-in chicken thighs with skin
- 1/4 tsp garlic salt
- 1/4 tsp onion salt
- 1/4 tsp dried oregano
- 1/4 tsp ground thyme
- 1/4 tsp paprika
- 1/4 tsp ground black pepper

Directions

- Get a casserole dish and then line it with foil and nonstick spray.
- Now set your oven to 350 degrees before doing anything else.

- Get a bowl, mix: pepper, garlic salt, paprika, onion salt, thyme, and oregano.
- Place your chicken in the dish and top with the spice mix.
- Cook everything in the oven for 65 mins.
- Enjoy.

Amount per serving (8 total)

Timing Information:

Preparation	10 m
Cooking	1 h
Total Time	1 h 10 m

Nutritional Information:

Calories	190 kcal
Fat	11.9 g
Carbohydrates	0.2g
Protein	19.2 g
Cholesterol	71 mg
Sodium	178 mg

* Percent Daily Values are based on a 2,000 calorie diet.

Chicken Thighs IX

(Indian Style I)

(Tandoori)

Ingredients

- 2 (6 oz.) containers plain yogurt
- 2 tsps kosher salt
- 1 tsp black pepper
- 1/2 tsp ground cloves
- 2 tbsps freshly grated ginger
- 3 cloves garlic, minced
- 4 tsps paprika
- 2 tsps ground cumin
- 2 tsps ground cinnamon
- 2 tsps ground coriander
- 16 chicken thighs
- olive oil spray

Directions

- Get a bowl, combine: garlic, ginger, paprika, yogurt, cumin, cloves, cinnamon, salt, coriander, and pepper.
- Clean your chicken pieces and then place them in the bowl with the yogurt.
- Coat the chicken evenly and place a covering on the bowl.
- Put everything in the fridge overnight.
- Grill your chicken pieces after topping them with some oil for 3 mins over direct heat, then flip and grill for 3 more mins.
- Place the chicken to the side of the grill over non direct heat and let it cook for 45 mins.
- Enjoy with cooked basmati rice.

Amount per serving (8 total)

Timing Information:

Preparation	10 m
Cooking	45 m
Total Time	8 h 55 m

Nutritional Information:

Calories	349 kcal
Fat	20.5 g
Carbohydrates	5.4g
Protein	34.2 g
Cholesterol	120 mg
Sodium	618 mg

* Percent Daily Values are based on a 2,000 calorie diet.

Chicken Thighs X (Japanese Style I)

Ingredients

- 1 tbsp cornstarch
- 1 tbsp cold water
- 1/2 C. white sugar
- 1/2 C. soy sauce
- 1/4 C. cider vinegar
- 1 clove garlic, minced
- 1/2 tsp ground ginger
- 1/4 tsp ground black pepper
- 12 skinless chicken thighs

Directions

- Get the following boiling with a medium to low level of heat: black pepper, cornstarch, ginger, water, vinegar, sugar, and soy sauce.

- Once the sauce is thick and has reduced a bit set your oven to 425 degrees before doing anything else.
- Enter your chicken into a casserole dish and top liberally with the thick sauce, then flip each piece and top with more sauce.
- Cook everything in the oven for 35 mins.
- Baste the chicken with the sauce every 7 mins.
- Enjoy.

Amount per serving (6 total)

Timing Information:

Preparation	30 m
Cooking	1 h
Total Time	1 h 30 m

Nutritional Information:

Calories	272 kcal
Fat	9.8 g
Carbohydrates	19.9g
Protein	24.7 g
Cholesterol	85 mg
Sodium	1282 mg

* Percent Daily Values are based on a 2,000 calorie diet.

Chicken Thighs XI

(Honey Mustard and Curry)

Ingredients

- 1 (3 lb) whole chicken, cut into pieces
- 1/2 C. butter, melted
- 1/2 C. honey
- 1/4 C. prepared mustard
- 1 tsp salt
- 1 tsp curry powder

Directions

- Set your oven to 350 degrees before doing anything else.
- Get a bowl, mix: curry, melted butter, salt, honey, and mustard.
- Enter your chicken into a casserole dish and then top everything with all the honey sauce.

- Cook the chicken in the oven for 80 mins.
- While the chicken is cooking baste it every 10 mins.
- Enjoy.

Amount per serving (6 total)

Timing Information:

Preparation	15 m
Cooking	1 h 15 m
Total Time	1 h 30 m

Nutritional Information:

Calories	514 kcal
Fat	32.9 g
Carbohydrates	24g
Protein	31.3 g
Cholesterol	138 mg
Sodium	709 mg

* Percent Daily Values are based on a 2,000 calorie diet.

Chicken Thighs XII

(Soy Sauce and Parsley)

Ingredients

- 1/2 C. butter
- 3 tbsps minced garlic
- 3 tbsps soy sauce
- 1/4 tsp black pepper
- 1 tbsp dried parsley
- 6 boneless chicken thighs, with skin
- dried parsley, to taste

Directions

- Get a casserole dish or broiler pan and coat it with oil or nonstick spray.
- Now turn on your ovens broiler to low if possible before doing anything else.

- Get a bowl, combine: parsley, butter, pepper, garlic, and soy sauce.
- Place it in the microwave for 3 mins.
- Place your chicken in the dish and top the chicken with the microwave mix.
- Leave some of the mix for basting during the cooking time.
- Cook the chicken under the broiler for 25 mins and turn the chicken half way through the cooking time.
- Now baste the chicken with the rest of the mix.
- Before serving add a garnishing of parsley.
- Enjoy.

Amount per serving (6 total)

Timing Information:

Preparation	10 m
Cooking	20 m
Total Time	30 m

Nutritional Information:

Calories	303 kcal
Fat	25.1 g
Carbohydrates	2.3g
Protein	16.8 g
Cholesterol	99 mg
Sodium	615 mg

* Percent Daily Values are based on a 2,000 calorie diet.

Chicken Thighs XIII

(Red Potatoes and Parsley)

Ingredients

- 8 chicken thighs
- 6 small red potatoes, quartered
- 1/2 C. extra-virgin olive oil, or as needed
- 1 tbsp chopped fresh rosemary
- 1 1/2 tsps chopped fresh oregano
- 1 1/2 tsps garlic powder
- salt and pepper to taste

Directions

- Set your oven to 375 degrees before doing anything else.
- Get a bowl, add in: potatoes, chicken, and olive oil.
- Place everything into a casserole dish and top with: pepper,

rosemary, salt, garlic powder, and oregano.
- Cook everything in the oven for 65 mins with a covering of foil around the dish and then 10 mins with no cover.
- Enjoy.

Amount per serving (6 total)

Timing Information:

Preparation	15 m
Cooking	1 h
Total Time	1 h 15 m

Nutritional Information:

Calories	497 kcal
Fat	31.9 g
Carbohydrates	27.6g
Protein	24.4 g
Cholesterol	78 mg
Sodium	81 mg

* Percent Daily Values are based on a 2,000 calorie diet.

Chicken Thighs XIV

(Indian Style II)

(Makhani)

(Butter Chicken)

Ingredients

- 1 tbsp peanut oil
- 1 shallot, finely chopped
- 1/4 white onion, chopped
- 2 tbsps butter
- 2 tsps lemon juice
- 1 tbsp ginger garlic paste
- 1 tsp garam masala
- 1 tsp chili powder
- 1 tsp ground cumin
- 1 bay leaf
- 1/4 C. plain yogurt
- 1 C. half-and-half
- 1 C. tomato puree
- 1/4 tsp cayenne pepper, or to taste

- 1 pinch salt
- 1 pinch black pepper
- 1 tbsp peanut oil
- 1 lb boneless, skinless chicken thighs, cut into bite-size pieces
- 1 tsp garam masala
- 1 pinch cayenne pepper
- 1 tbsp cornstarch
- 1/4 C. water

Directions

- Stir fry your onions and shallots in oil for 2 mins then add in: bay leaf, butter, cumin, lemon juice, chili powder, ginger-garlic paste, garam masala.
- Cook for 1 more min before adding: yoghurt and half and half.
- Get everything boiling and then gently simmer with a low level of heat for 12 mins while stirring.
- Now add in pepper and salt.

- Place the mix to the side and get a new pan.
- Add in 1 tbsp of oil and brown your chicken in the oil for 12 mins. Now lower the heat, and add in 1 tsp of masala and cayenne and a few tbsps of sauce.
- Let the chicken lightly boil in the sauce until fully done.
- Now add in the rest of the sauce.
- Finally combine in some water and cornstarch and cook everything for 12 mins until it all becomes thick.
- Enjoy.

Amount per serving (4 total)

Timing Information:

Preparation	10 m
Cooking	25 m
Total Time	35 m

Nutritional Information:

Calories	408 kcal
Fat	27.8 g
Carbohydrates	15.6g
Protein	23.4 g
Cholesterol	107 mg
Sodium	523 mg

* Percent Daily Values are based on a 2,000 calorie diet.

Chicken Thighs XV

(Mexican Fajitas)

Ingredients

- 1 tbsp Worcestershire sauce
- 1 tbsp cider vinegar
- 1 tbsp soy sauce
- 1 tsp chili powder
- 1 clove garlic, minced
- 1 dash hot pepper sauce
- 1 1/2 lbs boneless, skinless chicken thighs, cut into strips
- 1 tbsp vegetable oil
- 1 onion, thinly sliced
- 1 green bell pepper, sliced
- 1/2 lemon, juiced

Directions

- Get a bowl, combine: hot sauce, Worcestershire, chicken, garlic,

vinegar, chili powder, and soy sauce.
- Make sure the chicken pieces are evenly covered then place some plastic around the bowl.
- Let the chicken sit in the sauce for 40 mins on the counter or in the fridge.
- Stir fry your chicken pieces for 7 mins then combine in the green peppers and onions. Cook for 4 more mins and garnish the meat with some lemon.
- Serve with warmed tortillas.
- Enjoy.

Amount per serving (5 total)

Timing Information:

Preparation	15 m
Cooking	10 m
Total Time	55 m

Nutritional Information:

Calories	210 kcal
Fat	8.3 g
Carbohydrates	5.7g
Protein	27.6 g
Cholesterol	113 mg
Sodium	344 mg

* Percent Daily Values are based on a 2,000 calorie diet.

Chicken Thighs XVI

(Fried and Baked)

Ingredients

- 12 chicken thighs
- 3 eggs
- 1 C. all-purpose flour
- 1 C. Italian seasoned bread crumbs
- salt and pepper to taste
- 1 tsp paprika
- 1/2 C. vegetable oil

Directions

- Set your oven to 350 degrees before doing anything else.
- Get a bowl, add in: flour, pepper, and salt.
- Get a 2nd bowl, add: bread crumbs.

- Get a 3rd bowl for your whisked eggs.
- Dip the chicken in the flour, then into the eggs, and finally in the bread crumbs.
- Get a casserole dish and add in the oil and then the chicken and top with paprika.
- Cook everything in the oven for 35 mins then flip the chicken and continue cooking for 30 more mins.
- Place the chicken on paper towels for 10 mins before serving.
- Enjoy.

Amount per serving (10 total)

Timing Information:

Preparation	10 m
Cooking	1 h 30 m
Total Time	1 h 40 m

Nutritional Information:

Calories	310 kcal
Fat	15.1 g
Carbohydrates	18g
Protein	23.8 g
Cholesterol	126 mg
Sodium	296 mg

* Percent Daily Values are based on a 2,000 calorie diet.

Chicken Thighs XVII

(Japanese Style II)

Ingredients

- 1 C. soy sauce
- 1 C. brown sugar
- 1 C. water
- 4 cloves garlic, minced
- 1 onion, chopped
- 1 tbsp grated fresh ginger root
- 1 tbsp ground black pepper
- 1 tbsp dried oregano
- 1 tsp crushed red pepper flakes (optional)
- 1 tsp ground cayenne pepper (optional)
- 1 tsp ground paprika (optional)
- 5 lbs skinless chicken thighs

Directions

- Get a bowl, combine: paprika, soy sauce, cayenne, sugar, pepper flakes, water, oregano, garlic, black pepper, onions, and ginger.
- Now add the chicken and stir everything.
- Place a covering on the bowl, and place it in the fridge for 60 mins.
- Grill your chicken pieces for 16 mins each side.
- Enjoy.

Amount per serving (12 total)

Timing Information:

Preparation	
Cooking	30 m
Total Time	1 h 30 m

Nutritional Information:

Calories	338 kcal
Fat	12.6 g
Carbohydrates	21.7g
Protein	33.4 g
Cholesterol	114 mg
Sodium	1304 mg

* Percent Daily Values are based on a 2,000 calorie diet.

Chicken Thighs XVIII

(Spanish Style)

Ingredients

- 1 tbsp olive oil
- 3 lbs skinless chicken thighs
- salt and ground black pepper to taste
- 1/4 C. loosely packed cilantro leaves
- 2 large sweet potatoes, cut into chunks
- 1 red bell pepper, cut into strips
- 2 (15.5 oz.) cans black beans, rinsed and drained
- 1/2 C. chicken broth
- 1/4 C. loosely packed cilantro leaves
- 1 C. hot salsa
- 2 tsps ground cumin
- 1/2 tsp ground allspice
- 3 large cloves garlic, chopped
- lime wedges, for garnish

Directions

- Top your chicken pieces with pepper, 1/4 cilantro, and salt before browning them in olive oil for 6 mins per side.
- Place the chicken pieces in the crock pot as well as: black beans, garlic, broth, allspice, 1/4 cilantro, cumin, salsa, potatoes, and bell peppers.
- Cook everything on low for 5 hrs then garnish with some lime.
- Enjoy.

Amount per serving (6 total)

Timing Information:

Preparation	25 m
Cooking	4 h 10 m
Total Time	4 h 35 m

Nutritional Information:

Calories	591 kcal
Fat	18.1 g
Carbohydrates	56.9g
Protein	50.2 g
Cholesterol	1137 mg
Sodium	980 mg

* Percent Daily Values are based on a 2,000 calorie diet.

Chicken Thighs XIX

(Soy Sauce, Honey, and Basil)

Ingredients

- 4 skinless, boneless chicken thighs
- 1/2 C. soy sauce
- 1/2 C. ketchup
- 1/3 C. honey
- 3 cloves garlic, minced
- 1 tsp dried basil

Directions

- Get a bowl, mix: basil, soy sauce, garlic, ketchup, and honey.
- Add your chicken to the slow cooker as well as the honey sauce and cook for 6 hours with a low level of heat.
- Enjoy.

Amount per serving (4 total)

Timing Information:

Preparation	10 m
Cooking	6 h
Total Time	6 h 10 m

Nutritional Information:

Calories	325 kcal
Fat	11.9 g
Carbohydrates	34.2g
Protein	21.9 g
Cholesterol	71 mg
Sodium	2204 mg

* Percent Daily Values are based on a 2,000 calorie diet.

Chicken Thighs XX

(Maggie's Easy Sesame Chicken)

Ingredients

- 4 C. vegetable oil for frying
- 1 egg
- 1 1/2 lbs boneless, skinless chicken thighs, cut into 1/2 inch cubes
- 1 tsp salt
- 1 tsp white sugar
- 1 pinch white pepper
- 1 C. cornstarch
- 2 tbsps vegetable oil
- 3 tbsps chopped green onion
- 1 clove garlic, minced
- 6 dried whole red chilies
- 1 strip orange zest
- 1/2 C. white sugar
- 1/4 tsp ground ginger
- 3 tbsps chicken broth

- 1 tbsp rice vinegar
- 1/4 C. soy sauce
- 2 tsps sesame oil
- 2 tbsps peanut oil
- 2 tsps cornstarch
- 1/4 C. water
- 2 tbsps sesame seeds

Directions

- Get your oil to 375 degrees in a big pan before doing anything else
- Get a bowl, combine: white pepper, whisked eggs, salt, and chicken.
- Add in the cornstarch 1 tsp at a time and stir constantly.
- Fry your chicken, in batches, until golden in the oil for about 4 mins each.
- Then place everything to the side.
- Once all the batches have been fried.

- Fry them again for 1 to 2 mins each.
- Then place the fried pieces on some paper towels.
- Get another pan and add in 2 tbsps of veggie oil and stir fry the following in it for 3 mins: orange zest, green onions, chilies, and garlic.
- Now add in: peanut oil, half a C. of sugar, sesame oil, ginger, soy sauce, broth, and vinegar.
- Get everything boiling and let it cook for 4 mins.
- Add in 2 tsps of cornstarch with some water and then add this to the sauce and get it boiling again for 2 more mins.
- Add the chicken in, set the heat to low, and let the sauce combine into the chicken.
- Let everything cook for about 2 more mins then top with sesame seeds.
- Enjoy.

Amount per serving (6 total)

Timing Information:

Preparation	25 m
Cooking	25 m
Total Time	50 m

Nutritional Information:

Calories	634 kcal
Fat	36.5 g
Carbohydrates	54.9g
Protein	24.3 g
Cholesterol	101 mg
Sodium	1192 mg

* Percent Daily Values are based on a 2,000 calorie diet.

Chicken Thighs XXI

(BBQ)

Ingredients

- 4 tbsps water
- 3 tbsps ketchup
- 3 tbsps brown sugar
- 2 tbsps vinegar
- 1 tbsp lemon juice
- 2 tbsps Worcestershire sauce
- 1 tsp salt
- 1 tsp dry mustard
- 1 tsp chili powder
- 12 chicken thighs, skin removed

Directions

- Set your oven to 500 degrees before doing anything else.
- Get the following boiling for 2 mins: chili powder, water, mustard powder, ketchup, salt,

sugar, Worcestershire, vinegar, and lemon juice.
- Once everything is boiling reduce the heat and let it gently cook for 17 mins.
- Add your chicken to a casserole dish and top it with the sauce.
- Place a covering of foil around the dish and cook everything the oven for 17 mins.
- Now set the heat to 200 degrees and cook for 65 more mins.
- Take off the cover and finally let the chicken cook for 10 more mins to get crunchy.
- Enjoy.

Amount per serving (12 total)

Timing Information:

Preparation	20 m
Cooking	1 h 30 m
Total Time	1 h 50 m

Nutritional Information:

Calories	135 kcal
Fat	7.3 g
Carbohydrates	5.1g
Protein	11.8 g
Cholesterol	43 mg
Sodium	306 mg

* Percent Daily Values are based on a 2,000 calorie diet.

Chicken Thighs XXII

(Hawaiian Style)

Ingredients

- 1 tbsp vegetable oil
- 10 boneless, skinless chicken thighs
- 3/4 C. honey
- 3/4 C. lite soy sauce
- 3 tbsps ketchup
- 2 cloves garlic, crushed
- 1 tbsp minced fresh ginger root
- 1 (20 oz.) can pineapple tidbits, drained with juice reserved
- 2 tbsps cornstarch
- 1/4 C. water

Directions

- Get a bowl, combine: pineapple juice, honey, ginger, soy sauce, garlic, and ketchup.

- Brown your chicken for about 5 mins per side, in oil, then add them to your slow cooker. Now top everything with pineapple sauce.
- With a high level of heat let this cook for 4 hrs then take out the thighs, add in the pineapple and mix in the water and cornstarch. Let the sauce get thick.
- When serving your chicken top liberally with sauce.
- Enjoy.

Amount per serving (10 total)

Timing Information:

Preparation	20 m
Cooking	4 h
Total Time	4 h 20 m

Nutritional Information:

Calories	235 kcal
Fat	6 g
Carbohydrates	34.4g
Protein	13 g
Cholesterol	42 mg
Sodium	724 mg

* Percent Daily Values are based on a 2,000 calorie diet.

Chicken Thighs XXIII

(Indian Style III)

(Makhani)

(Slow Cooker)

Ingredients

- 2 tbsps butter
- 2 tbsps vegetable oil
- 4 large skinless, boneless chicken thighs, cut into bite-sized pieces
- 1 onion, diced
- 3 cloves garlic, minced
- 2 tsps curry powder
- 1 tbsp curry paste
- 2 tsps tandoori masala
- 1 tsp garam masala
- 1 (6 oz.) can tomato paste
- 15 green cardamom pods
- 1 C. low-fat plain yogurt
- 1 (14 oz.) can coconut milk
- salt to taste

Directions

- Stir fry your garlic, onions, and chicken in veggie oil and butter for 12 mins then add in: tomato paste, curry powder and paste, garam masala, and tandoori masala.
- Cook and stir fry, the mix for 3 mins until smooth, then add everything into your slow cooker.
- Add in: yogurt, cardamom, and coconut milk as well as pepper and salt to the mix and cook everything for 8 hrs on low.
- Enjoy with basmati rice.

Amount per serving (6 total)

Timing Information:

Preparation	15 m
Cooking	4 h 15 m
Total Time	4 h 30 m

Nutritional Information:

Calories	480 kcal
Fat	33.3 g
Carbohydrates	17.2g
Protein	30.6 g
Cholesterol	103 mg
Sodium	442 mg

* Percent Daily Values are based on a 2,000 calorie diet.

Chicken Thighs XXIV

(Arabic and Latin Fusion)

Ingredients

- 2 tbsps vegetable oil
- 1 onion, grated
- 2 cloves garlic, chopped
- 1 1/2 lbs boneless skinless chicken thighs, cut in half
- 3 tsps ground turmeric
- 1 tsp chili powder
- 1 1/2 tsps salt
- 1 (14.5 oz.) can peeled and diced tomatoes
- 2 tbsps ghee (clarified butter)
- 3 tsps ground cumin
- 3 tsps ground coriander
- 2 tbsps grated fresh ginger root
- 1/2 C. chopped cilantro leaves

Directions

- Stir fry your garlic and onions for 4 mins in oil then combine in the salt, tomatoes, chicken, chili powder, and turmeric.
- Get everything boiling, place a lid on the pan, set the heat to low, and cook for 22 mins.
- Remove the lid and cook the contents for 12 more mins to let most of the liquid cook out.
- Combine in: cilantro, ghee, ginger, cumin, and coriander.
- Now cook the mix for 6 more mins before serving with a topping of sauce.
- Enjoy.

Amount per serving (6 total)

Timing Information:

Preparation	20 m
Cooking	55 m
Total Time	1 h 15 m

Nutritional Information:

Calories	265 kcal
Fat	16.9 g
Carbohydrates	6.7g
Protein	20.4 g
Cholesterol	79 mg
Sodium	755 mg

* Percent Daily Values are based on a 2,000 calorie diet.

Chicken Thighs XXV

(Bacon and Potatoes)

Ingredients

- 6 chicken thighs
- 6 chicken drumsticks
- 12 slices center-cut bacon
- salt and black pepper to taste
- 1 onion, coarsely chopped
- 1 1/2 lbs baby Dutch yellow potatoes

Spice Mix:

- 2 tbsps dried chives
- 2 tbsps dried basil
- 1 tbsp garlic powder
- 1 tbsp adobo seasoning
- 1 tbsp ground black pepper
- 1 tsp salt, or to taste

Directions

- Set your oven to 400 degrees before doing anything else.
- Get your chicken and cover it with a piece of bacon then layer your chicken pieces in a casserole dish after topping them with onions, pepper, and salt.
- Get a bowl, mix: black pepper, chives, adobo, basil, and garlic powder.
- Add the potatoes around the chicken in the casserole dish and top everything with the chive spice mix.
- Cook the chicken and potatoes in the oven for 65 mins then top with more salt.
- Enjoy.

Amount per serving (6 total)

Timing Information:

Preparation	20 m
Cooking	1 h
Total Time	1 h 20 m

Nutritional Information:

Calories	548 kcal
Fat	27.7 g
Carbohydrates	24.6g
Protein	48.2 g
Cholesterol	155 mg
Sodium	1012 mg

* Percent Daily Values are based on a 2,000 calorie diet.

Chicken Thighs XXVI

(Jalapenos, Peanuts, and Ginger)

Ingredients

- 3/4 C. dark brown sugar
- 1/3 C. cold water
- 1/3 C. fish sauce
- 1/3 C. rice vinegar
- 1 tbsp soy sauce
- 4 cloves garlic, crushed
- 1 tbsp fresh grated ginger
- 1 tsp vegetable oil
- 8 boneless, skinless chicken thighs, quartered
- 1/2 C. roasted peanuts
- 2 fresh jalapeno peppers, seeded and sliced
- 1 bunch green onions, chopped
- fresh cilantro sprigs, for garnish

Directions

- Get a bowl, combine: ginger, brown sugar, garlic, water, soy sauce, vinegar, and fish sauce.
- Stir fry your chicken, in oil, for 3 mins, then add in 1/3 of a C. of the ginger mix, and cook for 8 mins until thick.
- Now add in the rest of the mix and cook for 7 more mins until the chicken is fully done.
- Once it is done add: onions, jalapenos, and peanuts.
- Heat everything for 4 mins then top everything with some cilantro.
- Enjoy.

Amount per serving (4 total)

Timing Information:

Preparation	20 m
Cooking	20 m
Total Time	40 m

Nutritional Information:

Calories	615 kcal
Fat	33.2 g
Carbohydrates	37.9g
Protein	43 g
Cholesterol	129 mg
Sodium	1967 mg

* Percent Daily Values are based on a 2,000 calorie diet.

Chicken Thighs XXVII

(Buttery Mushroom Bake)

Ingredients

- 8 chicken thighs
- 1 (10.75 oz.) can condensed cream of mushroom soup
- 10 oz. milk
- 1 tsp dried parsley
- 1/2 tsp onion powder
- 1 C. dry bread crumbs
- 2 tbsps melted butter
- 1 tsp cornstarch

Directions

- Set your oven to 350 degrees before doing anything else.
- Get a bowl, add in: soup, milk, onion powder, and parsley.
- Get a 2nd bowl for the bread crumbs.

- Coat the chicken with the milk mix and then some bread crumbs.
- Put everything into a casserole dish that has been coated with nonstick spray.
- Top the chicken with the butter and cook it all in the oven for 50 mins.
- Simultaneously combine the cornstarch and the rest of the soup in a small pan and stir until boiling. Once it is boiling, set the heat to low and cook for 3 mins until it becomes thick.
- Garnish your chicken with the hot soup mix.
- Enjoy.

Amount per serving (4 total)

Timing Information:

Preparation	15 m
Cooking	45 m
Total Time	1 h

Nutritional Information:

Calories	575 kcal
Fat	32.7 g
Carbohydrates	29g
Protein	39 g
Cholesterol	138 mg
Sodium	868 mg

* Percent Daily Values are based on a 2,000 calorie diet.

Chicken Thighs XXVIII

(Sunbelt Classic)

Ingredients

- 3 lbs chicken thighs
- 2 tbsps soy sauce
- 1/2 C. ketchup
- 1/4 C. corn syrup
- 1 pinch garlic powder

Directions

- Set your oven to 350 degrees before doing anything else.
- Get a bowl, combine: garlic powder, soy sauce, corn syrup, and ketchup.
- Clean your chicken and then place all the pieces in a casserole dish.
- Now top everything with the soy mix.

- Cook the chicken in the oven for 65 mins.
- Baste the meat at least 3 times before it finishes cooking.
- Enjoy.

Amount per serving (4 total)

Timing Information:

Preparation	10 m
Cooking	1 h
Total Time	1 h 10 m

Nutritional Information:

Calories	807 kcal
Fat	52 g
Carbohydrates	23.1g
Protein	59.9 g
Cholesterol	1286 mg
Sodium	1044 mg

* Percent Daily Values are based on a 2,000 calorie diet.

Chicken Thighs XXVIII

(Creamy Onions)

(Slow Cooker)

Ingredients

- 8 skinless, boneless chicken thighs halves
- 4 potatoes, cubed
- 1 (10.75 oz.) can condensed cream of mushroom soup
- 1 1/3 C. milk
- 1 tbsp cornstarch
- 1 (1 oz.) package dry onion soup mix

Directions

- Get a bowl, mix: soup mix, mushroom soup, cornstarch, and milk.

- Add the potatoes to the crock pot as well as the chicken.
- Top the chicken with the soup mix.
- Place a lid on the slow cooker and let it cook for 9 hrs with a low level of heat.
- Enjoy.

Amount per serving (5 total)

Timing Information:

Preparation	10 m
Cooking	10 h
Total Time	10 h 10 m

Nutritional Information:

Calories	444 kcal
Fat	7.5 g
Carbohydrates	41.9g
Protein	50.5 g
Cholesterol	1115 mg
Sodium	1048 mg

* Percent Daily Values are based on a 2,000 calorie diet.

Chicken Thighs XXX

(Chicken and Rice)

Ingredients

- 2 cubes chicken bouillon
- 1 tbsp water
- 1 C. uncooked white rice
- 1/4 C. butter
- 1 onion, chopped
- 2 C. water
- 6 chicken thighs
- 1 tsp Italian-style seasoning

Directions

- Set your oven to 350 degrees before doing anything else.
- Get a bowl, mix: 2 C. of water, onion, bouillon, butter, and rice.
- Layer the rice, once it has been stirred into a casserole dish then place your chicken on top.

- Add some pepper and salt to the chicken and cook everything for 50 mins in the oven.
- Enjoy.

Amount per serving (6 total)

Timing Information:

Preparation	10 m
Cooking	50 m
Total Time	1 h

Nutritional Information:

Calories	394 kcal
Fat	22.3 g
Carbohydrates	28g
Protein	18.9 g
Cholesterol	100 mg
Sodium	513 mg

* Percent Daily Values are based on a 2,000 calorie diet.

Chicken Thighs XXXI

(Easy Sweet Bake)

Ingredients

- 1 (3 lb) whole chicken, cut into pieces
- 1/2 C. ketchup
- 1/4 C. water
- 1/4 C. packed brown sugar
- 1 (1 oz.) package dry onion soup mix

Directions

- Set your oven to 350 degrees before doing anything else.
- Get a bowl, mix: soup mix, ketchup, sugar, and water.
- Layer the chicken in a casserole dish.
- Top with the soup mix.

- Cook the mix in the oven for 65 mins.
- Enjoy.

Amount per serving (6 total)

Timing Information:

Preparation	10 m
Cooking	1 h
Total Time	1 h 10 m

Nutritional Information:

Calories	555 kcal
Fat	34.3 g
Carbohydrates	16.9g
Protein	42.9 g
Cholesterol	170 mg
Sodium	797 mg

* Percent Daily Values are based on a 2,000 calorie diet.

Chicken Thighs XXXII

(Italian Style)

Ingredients

- 4 lbs dark meat chicken pieces
- 1 tbsp vegetable oil
- 5 cloves crushed garlic
- 1/2 C. all-purpose flour
- 1 tsp poultry seasoning
- 3 (4 oz.) links sweet Italian sausage, sliced
- 1 C. chopped onion
- 3 carrots, sliced
- 1/2 lb fresh mushrooms, sliced
- 1/2 tsp dried rosemary
- 1 C. red wine
- 1 (14.5 oz.) can whole peeled tomatoes
- salt and pepper to taste

Directions

- Get a bowl, combine: poultry seasoning and flour. Then coat the chicken with this mix.
- Stir fry half of your garlic in oil for 2 mins.
- Then brown the chicken in the oil for 5 mins before adding in the sausage and cooking for 2 more mins.
- Now add: the rest of garlic, onions, tomatoes, rosemary, carrots, wine, and mushrooms.
- Get everything boiling, once it is boiling, place a lid on the pan, set the heat to low, and cook the contents for 30 mins.
- Add in some pepper and salt and cook for 12 more mins.
- Let the chicken sit for 13 mins before serving.
- Enjoy.

Amount per serving (8 total)

Timing Information:

Preparation	10 m
Cooking	50 m
Total Time	1 h

Nutritional Information:

Calories	616 kcal
Fat	36.9 g
Carbohydrates	20.4g
Protein	43.5 g
Cholesterol	150 mg
Sodium	519 mg

* Percent Daily Values are based on a 2,000 calorie diet.

Chicken Thighs XXXIII

(Indian Style IV)

Ingredients

- 1 large onion, chopped
- 4 cloves garlic, chopped
- 1 slice fresh ginger root
- 1 tbsp olive oil
- 2 tsps ground cumin
- 1 tsp ground turmeric
- 1 tsp salt
- 1 tsp ground black pepper
- 1/2 tsp ground cardamom
- 1 (1 inch) piece cinnamon stick
- 1/4 tsp ground cloves
- 2 bay leaves
- 1/4 tsp ground nutmeg
- 6 skinless chicken thighs
- 1 (14.5 oz.) can whole peeled tomatoes, crushed

Directions

- In a blender puree: ginger, garlic, and onions.
- Then stir fry this mix in oil for 12 mins.
- Add in: nutmeg, cumin, bay leaves, turmeric, cloves, salt, cinnamon, pepper, and cardamom.
- Cook for 2 more mins before adding the chicken.
- Coat the chicken pieces with the spices and cook for 5 mins before adding the tomatoes and their juice.
- Get everything boiling, set the heat to low, and cook for 90 mins.
- Cook this with a lid on the pot.
- Enjoy.

Amount per serving (6 total)

Timing Information:

Preparation	15 m
Cooking	2 h
Total Time	2 h 15 m

Nutritional Information:

Calories	134 kcal
Fat	5.4 g
Carbohydrates	6.9g
Protein	14.7 g
Cholesterol	57 mg
Sodium	547 mg

* Percent Daily Values are based on a 2,000 calorie diet.

Chicken Thighs XXXIV

(Lemons and Oregano)

Ingredients

- 7 chicken thighs
- 2 tsps dried oregano
- salt and pepper to taste
- 1/4 C. olive oil
- 1/2 lemon, juiced

Directions

- Set your oven to 450 degrees before doing anything else.
- Clean your chicken then top with pepper, salt, and oregano then layer the pieces into a casserole dish coated with nonstick spray.
- Get a bowl, combine: lemon juice and oil.
- Coat the chicken with half of the mix.

- Cook everything in the oven for 20 mins.
- Now flip the pieces and top the contents with the rest of the lemon mix.
- Cook the dish for 20 more mins in the oven.
- Enjoy.

Amount per serving (7 total)

Timing Information:

Preparation	10 m
Cooking	50 m
Total Time	1 h 10 m

Nutritional Information:

Calories	269 kcal
Fat	22.1 g
Carbohydrates	1.1g
Protein	16.4 g
Cholesterol	79 mg
Sodium	72 mg

* Percent Daily Values are based on a 2,000 calorie diet.

Chicken Thighs XXXV

(Buttery Garlic and Prosciutto)

Ingredients

- 2 tbsps butter or margarine, melted
- 6 chicken thighs
- salt and pepper to taste
- 6 slices prosciutto (thin sliced)
- 2 tbsps minced garlic, divided
- 1 C. sliced fresh mushrooms
- 1/4 C. dry white wine (optional)
- 1 C. sour cream

Directions

- Set your oven to 350 degrees before doing anything else.
- Top your chicken pieces with: 1 tbsp of garlic, pepper, and salt.

- Cover them with a wrapping of prosciutto.
- Coat your baking dish with some melted butter and then layer your chicken pieces in it.
- Now top everything with the rest of the garlic and the mushrooms.
- Cook the chicken and mushrooms in the oven for 65 mins.
- Add the liquid from the baking dish into a pot and add in sour cream and wine in it.
- Cook everything simmering for about 6 mins.
- Garnish your chicken liberally with the sauce when serving.
- Enjoy.

Amount per serving (6 total)

Timing Information:

Preparation	10 m
Cooking	1 h
Total Time	1 h 10 m

Nutritional Information:

Calories	383 kcal
Fat	30.8 g
Carbohydrates	3.3g
Protein	20.7 g
Cholesterol	119 mg
Sodium	399 mg

* Percent Daily Values are based on a 2,000 calorie diet.

Chicken Thighs XXXVI

(Louisiana Style)

(Gumbo)

Ingredients

- 2 tbsps butter
- 2 cloves garlic
- 2 C. chopped onion
- 1/2 C. chopped green bell pepper
- 1/2 C. chopped celery
- 1 lb okra, chopped
- 1/4 C. canola oil
- 1/4 C. all-purpose flour
- 1 lb chicken thighs
- 1 lb andouille sausage links
- 2 C. water
- 6 C. chicken broth
- 2 lbs fresh shrimp, peeled and deveined
- 1 sprig fresh thyme
- 3 tsps chopped fresh parsley
- 1/2 tsp salt

- 1/4 tsp cayenne pepper
- 1/2 tsp hot pepper sauce (e.g. Tabasco(TM))
- 1/2 tsp file powder (optional)

Directions

- Stir fry your: okra, garlic, celery, onions, and bell peppers in butter until brown.
- Then place it all into a bowl.
- Add in your sausage and brown them.
- Place the sausages to the side as well.
- Now add in veggie oil to the pan and fry the chicken for 22 mins, flipping them every so often.
- Once the chicken is done, place it in the bowl too.
- Add some flour to the pan and begin to stir the mix over a low level of heat and continue cooking and stirring for about 30 mins until it becomes brown now

add in water (two C.) as well as: pepper, garlic, and onions.
- Increase the heat and get everything boiling.
- Once everything is boiling add the broth and get it boiling again, now reduce the heat to low and let the mix simmer.
- Chunk your chicken and pour the pieces into the simmering broth. Now add the sausage and okra mix.
- Let this gently cook for 60 mins.
- Simultaneously boil your rice in 2 C. of water to a boil, then place a lid on the pot, and set the heat to a low level.
- Let the rice cook for 22 mins then add in the shrimp and: hot sauce, thyme, cayenne, parsley, and salt.
- Cook for 22 more mins before shutting the heat and adding in the file powder.
- Serve the rice with a topping of chicken, sausage and okra.
- Enjoy.

Amount per serving (10 total)

Timing Information:

Preparation	45 m
Cooking	3 h
Total Time	3 h 45 m

Nutritional Information:

Calories	435 kcal
Fat	27.7 g
Carbohydrates	11.3g
Protein	33.8 g
Cholesterol	202 mg
Sodium	1295 mg

* Percent Daily Values are based on a 2,000 calorie diet.

Chicken Thighs XXXVII

(Thai Style)

Ingredients

- 3 lemongrass stalks, bottom two-thirds of tender inner bulbs only, thinly sliced
- 4 cloves garlic, chopped
- 1 (4 inch) piece fresh ginger root, chopped
- 4 C. chicken broth
- 1 tbsp vegetable oil
- 2 1/2 lbs skinless, boneless chicken thighs, cut into chunks
- 12 oz. fresh white mushrooms, quartered
- 2 tsps red curry paste
- 3 tbsps fish sauce
- 1 lime, juiced
- 2 (14 oz.) cans coconut milk
- 1 red onion, sliced
- 1/2 bunch cilantro, roughly chopped

- 1 lime, cut into wedges, for serving
- 1 fresh jalapeno pepper, sliced into rings

Directions

- Get the following boiling: broth, lemon grass, ginger, and garlic.
- Set the heat to a low level and cook for 35 mins.
- Drain out the broth and place everything to the side, throw away the other contents.
- Get a big pot and stir fry your chicken for 7 mins in veggie oil then add the mushrooms and fry for 7 more mins.
- Now add: lime juice, curry paste, and fish sauce.
- Add the broth as well as the coconut milk.
- Get everything boiling, then lower the heat, and gently cook for 22 mins.

- Remove any excess oils then add in the onions and cook for 7 more mins.
- Shut the heat and top the contents with some cilantro.
- Serve the soup with some jalapenos, more cilantro, and lime pieces.
- Enjoy.

Amount per serving (6 total)

Timing Information:

Preparation	15 m
Cooking	1 h
Total Time	1 h 15 m

Nutritional Information:

Calories	596 kcal
Fat	44.8 g
Carbohydrates	14.3g
Protein	41 g
Cholesterol	114 mg
Sodium	1207 mg

* Percent Daily Values are based on a 2,000 calorie diet.

Chicken Thighs XXXVIII

(Cream of Everything with Wine)

Ingredients

- 1 tbsp butter
- 8 skinless chicken thighs
- salt and pepper to taste
- 1 (10.75 oz.) can condensed cream of celery soup
- 1 (10.75 oz.) can condensed cream of mushroom soup
- 1 (5 oz.) jar pimento-stuffed green olives
- 1 (8 oz.) package sliced fresh mushrooms
- 1 1/4 C. Chablis wine
- 1 tbsp all-purpose flour

Directions

- Top your chicken with some pepper and salt then brown it all over in butter for 5 mins. Then add it into a crock pot.
- Cook your celery soup and mushroom soup in the same pan and heat it up for 3 mins.
- Then top the chicken with it.
- Add in the flour, olives, wine, and mushrooms to the slow cooker as well and stir everything evenly.
- Place a lid on the slow cooker and with low heat cook everything for 9 hrs.
- Enjoy.

Amount per serving (4 total)

Timing Information:

Preparation	25 m
Cooking	8 h
Total Time	8 h 25 m

Nutritional Information:

Calories	528 kcal
Fat	23.8 g
Carbohydrates	15.1g
Protein	49.9 g
Cholesterol	1207 mg
Sodium	2308 mg

* Percent Daily Values are based on a 2,000 calorie diet.

Chicken Thighs XXXIX

(Moroccan Style)

(Tagine)

(Slow Cooker)

Ingredients

- 2 tbsps olive oil
- 8 skinless, boneless chicken thighs, cut into 1-inch pieces
- 1 eggplant, cut into 1 inch cubes
- 2 large onions, thinly sliced
- 4 large carrots, thinly sliced
- 1/2 C. dried cranberries
- 1/2 C. chopped dried apricots
- 2 C. chicken broth
- 2 tbsps tomato paste
- 2 tbsps lemon juice
- 2 tbsps all-purpose flour
- 2 tsps garlic salt
- 1 1/2 tsps ground cumin
- 1 1/2 tsps ground ginger

- 1 tsp cinnamon
- 3/4 tsp ground black pepper
- 1 C. water
- 1 C. couscous

Directions

- Brown your chicken in olive oil along with the eggplants as well.
- Once everything is browned place the mix in the crock pot.
- Add the following to the chicken: apricots, onions, cranberries, and carrots.
- Get a bowl, combine: black pepper, broth, cinnamon, tomato paste, ginger, lemon juice, cumin, flour, and garlic salt.
- Add the wet mix to the slow cooker as well.
- Place a lid on the crock pot and cook the mix for 5 hrs on high.
- When 1 hour is left in the cooking time get your water boiling. Once it is boiling add in the couscous.

- Place a lid on the pot, and shut the heat.
- Let the couscous stand in the water for 7 mins. Then stir it.
- Serve the chicken on top of the couscous.
- Enjoy.

Amount per serving (8 total)

Timing Information:

Preparation	30 m
Cooking	5 h
Total Time	5 h 30 m

Nutritional Information:

Calories	380 kcal
Fat	15.2 g
Carbohydrates	38.5g
Protein	22.3 g
Cholesterol	65 mg
Sodium	571 mg

* Percent Daily Values are based on a 2,000 calorie diet.

Chicken Thighs XL
(Italian Style II)

Ingredients

- 15 chicken thighs
- 8 large potatoes, peeled and quartered
- 1 C. vegetable oil, or as needed
- 1/2 C. wine vinegar
- 5 lemons, juiced
- 10 cloves crushed garlic
- 2 tbsps dried oregano
- 2 tbsps dried parsley
- 1 onion, minced
- salt and pepper to taste

Directions

- Set your oven to 350 degrees before doing anything else.
- Fry your potatoes in oil until golden.

- Get a bowl, combine: half a C. of frying oil, vinegar, pepper, lemon juice, salt, garlic, onion, parsley, and oregano.
- Now layer your chicken in a casserole dish.
- Surround the chicken with the potatoes and then top the chicken with the wet mix.
- Cook everything in the oven for 80 mins.
- Baste the chicken at least 3 times throughout the cooking time.
- Enjoy.

Amount per serving (15 total)

Timing Information:

Preparation	15 m
Cooking	1 h 15 m
Total Time	1 h 30 m

Nutritional Information:

Calories	275 kcal
Fat	8.4 g
Carbohydrates	33.3g
Protein	19.1 g
Cholesterol	58 mg
Sodium	64 mg

* Percent Daily Values are based on a 2,000 calorie diet.

Chicken Thighs XLI

(Thai Style II)

Ingredients

- 1 C. soy sauce
- 8 cloves garlic, minced
- 1 tbsp minced fresh ginger root
- 2 tbsps hot pepper sauce
- 2 lbs skinless chicken thighs
- 1 tbsp sesame oil
- 1 tbsp brown sugar
- 1 onion, sliced
- 1/2 C. water
- 4 tbsps crunchy peanut butter
- 2 tbsps green onions, chopped

Directions

- Get a bowl, combine: hot sauce, soy sauce, chicken, ginger, and garlic.

- Cover the chicken pieces evenly with the mix and then place a covering over the bowl.
- Place everything in the fridge for 2 hours.
- Heat your sesame oil with some brown sugar in it until smooth then stir fry your onions in it for 7 mins.
- Combine in: the chicken and cook for 7 more mins flipping the chicken after 3 mins of frying.
- Add the marinade, and some water and get everything boiling.
- Once everything is boiling set the heat to low and let the contents cook for 22 mins. Now combine in the peanut butter and cook for 12 more mins.
- When serving your chicken top it liberally with sauce and also some chives.
- Enjoy.

Amount per serving (4 total)

Timing Information:

Preparation	20 m
Cooking	30 m
Total Time	50 m

Nutritional Information:

Calories	466 kcal
Fat	20.5 g
Carbohydrates	16.8g
Protein	53.4 g
Cholesterol	1188 mg
Sodium	3930 mg

* Percent Daily Values are based on a 2,000 calorie diet.

Chicken Thighs XLII

(Creole Style I)

Ingredients

- 8 chicken thighs
- 1/4 lb cooked ham, cut into one inch cubes
- 1 (16 oz.) can diced tomatoes
- 1 green bell pepper, chopped
- 6 green onions, chopped
- 1 (6 oz.) can tomato paste
- 1 tsp salt
- 2 dashes hot pepper sauce
- 2 C. water
- 1 C. uncooked long grain white rice
- 1/2 lb Polish sausage, sliced diagonally

Directions

- Put the following in your crock pot: hot sauce, chicken, salt, ham, tomato paste, tomatoes, onions, and bell peppers.
- Place a lid on the slow cooker and with low heat let the contents cook for 5 hrs.
- Get your rice and water boiling then place a lid on the pot, set the heat to low, and let it cook for 22 mins.
- Add the sausage and the rice to the crock pot and continue cooking for 40 mins with a high level of heat. At this point the sausage should be completely done.
- Enjoy.

Amount per serving (8 total)

Timing Information:

Preparation	15 m
Cooking	5 h 20 m
Total Time	5 h 35 m

Nutritional Information:

Calories	389 kcal
Fat	19.2 g
Carbohydrates	27.9g
Protein	24.5 g
Cholesterol	81 mg
Sodium	1083 mg

* Percent Daily Values are based on a 2,000 calorie diet.

Chicken Thighs XLIII

(Thai Style III)

Ingredients

- 3/4 C. hot salsa
- 1/4 C. chunky peanut butter
- 3/4 C. light coconut milk
- 2 tbsps lime juice
- 1 tbsp soy sauce
- 1 tsp white sugar
- 2 tbsps grated fresh ginger
- 2 lbs skinless chicken thighs
- 1/2 C. chopped peanuts, for topping
- 2 tbsps chopped cilantro, for topping

Directions

- Add the following to your slow cooker: ginger, salsa, sugar,

peanut butter, soy sauce, coconut milk, and lime juice.
- Add in the chicken as well and cook everything for 9 hours with a low level of heat.
- When serving the chicken add a topping of cilantro and peanuts.
- Enjoy.

Amount per serving (4 total)

Timing Information:

Preparation	15 m
Cooking	8 h
Total Time	8 h 15 m

Nutritional Information:

Calories	562 kcal
Fat	35.9 g
Carbohydrates	13.7g
Protein	47.6 g
Cholesterol	137 mg
Sodium	860 mg

* Percent Daily Values are based on a 2,000 calorie diet.

Chicken Thighs XLIV

(Chili Peppers and Monterey)

(Mexican Style)

Ingredients

- 15 boneless, skinless chicken thighs
- 1 (26 oz.) can condensed cream of chicken soup
- 2 cloves garlic, chopped (optional)
- 1 (16 oz.) container sour cream
- 1 (7 oz.) can diced green chili peppers
- 15 flour tortillas
- 3 1/2 C. shredded Monterey Jack cheese
- 1 (10 oz.) can sliced black olives (optional)
- chives for garnish (optional)
- black pepper to taste

Directions

- Boil your chicken in water for 12 mins. Then remove all the liquid and chunk the chicken when it is cool enough.
- Place everything into a bowl.
- Add to the chicken: chilies, soup, sour cream, and garlic.
- Coat your crock pot with nonstick spray then layer pieces of ripped tortillas at the bottom. Now layer half of the chicken mix, half of cheese, and then the soup over the tortillas.
- Continue layering until all of ingredients have been used up.
- Now add a final layering of olives.
- Cook the contents with a low level of heat for 5 hours.
- Enjoy.

Amount per serving (10 total)

Timing Information:

Preparation	30 m
Cooking	4 h
Total Time	4 h 30 m

Nutritional Information:

Calories	824 kcal
Fat	44 g
Carbohydrates	66.4g
Protein	40 g
Cholesterol	123 mg
Sodium	1931 mg

* Percent Daily Values are based on a 2,000 calorie diet.

Chicken Thighs XLV

(Vinegar and Salt)

(English Style)

Ingredients

- 2 C. cider vinegar
- 1 C. vegetable oil
- 1 egg, lightly beaten
- 3 tsps salt
- 1 tsp poultry seasoning
- 8 boneless chicken thighs, with skin

Directions

- Get a bowl, combine: poultry seasoning, chicken, vinegar, salt, veggie oil, and beaten eggs.
- Stir everything to coat the chicken and then place a covering

of plastic on the bowl and let it sit in the fridge for 2 hrs.
- Set your oven to 350 degrees before doing anything else.
- Layer your chicken pieces in a casserole dish and top them with half of the marinade.
- Cook everything in the oven for 35 mins then remove any liquids.
- Now cook for 17 more mins until the chicken is fully done and a bit crispy.
- Enjoy.

Amount per serving (8 total)

Timing Information:

Preparation	15 m
Cooking	45 m
Total Time	2 h

Nutritional Information:

Calories	418 kcal
Fat	37.6 g
Carbohydrates	0.7g
Protein	16.6 g
Cholesterol	82 mg
Sodium	937 mg

* Percent Daily Values are based on a 2,000 calorie diet.

Chicken Thighs XLVI

(Arabic Style)

Ingredients

- 1 tsp olive oil
- 1 C. sliced onion
- 2 1/2 lbs skinless, boneless chicken thighs
- 1 tbsp garam masala
- 1/2 tsp curry powder
- 1/2 C. red wine
- 2 tbsps red wine vinegar
- 1 C. fat-free, reduced-sodium chicken broth

Directions

- Stir fry your onions in olive oil for 9 mins then place them to the side.
- Turn up the heat and top your chicken with some curry and

masala before laying it in the pan and browning it for 5 mins.
- Now flip the chicken and cook it for 5 more mins.
- Add in the wine and vinegar and cook for 2 mins before scraping the bottom of the pan.
- Add the broth and onions and get everything boiling.
- Once it is boiling place a lid on the pot, set the heat to low, and let the contents gently simmer for 22 mins.
- Enjoy.

Amount per serving (6 total)

Timing Information:

Preparation	10 m
Cooking	35 m
Total Time	45 m

Nutritional Information:

Calories	331 kcal
Fat	19.7 g
Carbohydrates	3.6g
Protein	29.8 g
Cholesterol	106 mg
Sodium	95 mg

* Percent Daily Values are based on a 2,000 calorie diet.

Chicken Thighs XLVII (African Style)

Ingredients

- 12 chicken thighs
- 1 (12 oz.) jar hot chutney
- 1 (1 oz.) package dry onion soup mix

Directions

- Set your oven to 375 degrees before doing anything else.
- Get a bowl, combine: soup and chutney.
- Top your chicken with some pepper and salt and lay them into a casserole dish.
- Top the chicken pieces with your wet mix and cook them in the oven for 65 mins.

- Baste the chicken at least once with any drippings
- Enjoy.

Amount per serving (6 total)

Timing Information:

Preparation	10 m
Cooking	1 h 10 m
Total Time	1 h 20 m

Nutritional Information:

Calories	495 kcal
Fat	29 g
Carbohydrates	25g
Protein	33.5 g
Cholesterol	158 mg
Sodium	566 mg

* Percent Daily Values are based on a 2,000 calorie diet.

Chicken Thighs XLVIII

(Parsley, Peppers, and Sweet Onions)

Ingredients

- 3 tbsps vegetable oil
- 2 red bell peppers, seeded and diced
- 2 large sweet onions, peeled and cut into wedges
- 1 1/2 lbs skinless, boneless chicken boneless thighs - cut into cubes
- 2 cloves garlic, minced
- 1 pinch ground cayenne pepper
- 1 lemon, juiced
- 2 tbsps butter
- 2 tbsps chopped fresh parsley
- salt and pepper to taste

Directions

- Stir fry your onions and bell peppers in oil until tender then place them to the side.
- Combine the chicken into the pan and brown them before adding the red pepper and garlic.
- Cook for 3 mins with a low heat then add in lemon juice and scrape the bottom of the pan.
- Combine in your butter and let it melt.
- Now add the pepper mix back into the pan as well.
- Cook for about 4 more mins before topping with parsley and some pepper and salt.
- Enjoy.

Amount per serving (4 total)

Timing Information:

Preparation	10 m
Cooking	40 m
Total Time	1 h 10 m

Nutritional Information:

Calories	420 kcal
Fat	18.6 g
Carbohydrates	22.1g
Protein	42.2 g
Cholesterol	114 mg
Sodium	163 mg

* Percent Daily Values are based on a 2,000 calorie diet.

Chicken Thighs XLIX (Japanese Style III)

Ingredients

- 2 C. uncooked jasmine rice
- 4 C. water
- 4 skinless, boneless chicken thighs, cut into small pieces
- 1 onion, cut in half and sliced
- 2 C. dashi stock, made with dashi powder
- 1/4 C. soy sauce
- 3 tbsps mirin (Japanese rice wine)
- 3 tbsps brown sugar
- 4 eggs

Directions

- Run your rice under water then add them to 4 C. of fresh water in a pot and get it boiling.

- Once everything is boiling place a lid on the pot, set the heat to low, and let the contents simmer for 22 mins.
- Get a pan and coat it with nonstick spray.
- Cook your chicken until fully done, in the pan, while covered, for 7 mins, then add the onions and cook for 7 more mins.
- Add in the following: sugar, stock, mirin, and soy sauce.
- Get the mixture boiling while stirring and then let it thicken for about 9 to 12 mins.
- Beat your eggs and then add them to the stock.
- Place a lid on the pan and set the heat to low. Let the eggs poach for 7 mins or until cooked.
- Now shut the heat.
- Get a bowl for serving and add some rice, 1/4 of the chicken mix, and half a C. of soup.
- Enjoy.

Amount per serving (4 total)

Timing Information:

Preparation	15 m
Cooking	25 m
Total Time	40 m

Nutritional Information:

Calories	688 kcal
Fat	14.6 g
Carbohydrates	97.9g
Protein	35.3 g
Cholesterol	208 mg
Sodium	1226 mg

* Percent Daily Values are based on a 2,000 calorie diet.

Chicken Thighs L

(Cranberries and Onions)

Ingredients

- 6 chicken thighs
- 1 (16 oz.) can cranberry sauce
- 1 (8 oz.) bottle Russian-style salad dressing
- 1 packet dry onion soup mix

Directions

- Set your oven to 350 degrees before doing anything else.
- Get a bowl, combine: soup mix, dressing, and cranberry sauce.
- Coat a casserole dish with nonstick spray and layer your chicken pieces in it. Cover the chicken with the wet mix.

- Place some foil around the casserole dish and cook it in the oven for 90 mins.
- When 20 mins is left take off the foil and finish the baking.
- Enjoy.

Amount per serving (7 total)

Timing Information:

Preparation	15 m
Cooking	1 h 45 m
Total Time	2 h

Nutritional Information:

Calories	397 kcal
Fat	20.8 g
Carbohydrates	38.4g
Protein	15 g
Cholesterol	68 mg
Sodium	828 mg

* Percent Daily Values are based on a 2,000 calorie diet.

Easy Chicken Fry

Ingredients

- 1 (3 lb) whole chicken, cut into 6 pieces
- 2 eggs, beaten
- 1 (12 fluid oz.) can evaporated milk
- 2 tsps salt
- 2 tsps ground black pepper
- 2 tsps garlic powder
- 2 tsps onion powder
- 2 1/2 C. all-purpose flour
- 1 1/2 C. vegetable oil for frying

Directions

- Get a bowl mix: milk, onion powder, eggs, garlic powder, pepper, and salt.
- Get a 2nd bowl and add the flour to it.
- Coat the chicken first with the wet mix and then the dry flour.

- Now fry your chicken in hot oil for about 7 to 10 mins per side until it is fully done.
- Enjoy.

Amount per serving (6 total)

Timing Information:

Preparation	10 m
Cooking	20 m
Total Time	30 m

Nutritional Information:

Calories	638 kcal
Fat	29.6 g
Carbohydrates	47.9g
Protein	42.7 g
Cholesterol	177 mg
Sodium	960 mg

* Percent Daily Values are based on a 2,000 calorie diet.

Gumbo I

Ingredients

- 1 (3 lb) whole chicken
- 1/2 C. all-purpose flour
- 1/2 C. vegetable oil
- 1 (10 oz.) package frozen chopped onions
- 1 (10 oz.) package frozen green bell peppers
- 5 stalks celery, finely chopped
- 1 tbsp Cajun seasoning (such as Tony Chachere's), or to taste
- 2 whole bay leaves
- 1 (28 oz.) can diced tomatoes
- 1 lb fully-cooked smoked beef sausage (such as Hillshire Farm(R)), sliced
- 1 (10 oz.) package frozen sliced okra
- salt and black pepper to taste

Directions

- Boil your water and salt, then simmer your chicken in it for 1 hour until fully cooked.
- Take the chicken out from the water and cut it in half to cool faster.
- Keep the water the chicken was cooked in.
- Once the chicken is no longer hot take off the meat from the bones.
- Now get a big pan and mix: veggie oil and flour together to form a roux.
- Make this roux with a low level of heat and constantly stir it for about 22 mins until it becomes brown.
- Once it is brown add in: bay leaves, onions, Cajun seasoning, celery and bell peppers.
- Again with a low heat let the veggies simmer for 40 mins.
- Now add the chicken broth (the boiled water), sausage, and diced tomatoes.
- Let the contents simmer for 1 more hour.

- Now add in your meat from the chicken and your okra and let everything simmer for 50 more mins.
- Enjoy your gumbo.

Amount per serving (10 total)

Timing Information:

Preparation	20 m
Cooking	3 h 15 m
Total Time	3 h 55 m

Nutritional Information:

Calories	437 kcal
Fat	32.2 g
Carbohydrates	14.5g
Protein	21.4 g
Cholesterol	67 mg
Sodium	873 mg

* Percent Daily Values are based on a 2,000 calorie diet.

Jambalaya I

Ingredients

- 1 lb skinless, boneless chicken breast halves - cut into 1 inch cubes
- 1 lb andouille sausage, sliced
- 1 (28 oz.) can diced tomatoes with juice
- 1 large onion, chopped
- 1 large green bell pepper, chopped
- 1 C. chopped celery
- 1 C. chicken broth
- 2 tsps dried oregano
- 2 tsps dried parsley
- 2 tsps Cajun seasoning
- 1 tsp cayenne pepper
- 1/2 tsp dried thyme
- 1 lb frozen cooked shrimp without tails

Directions

- Cook the following on low for 8 hours in your slow cooker: thyme, chicken, cayenne, sausage, Cajun seasoning, tomatoes and juice, parsley, onions, oregano, bell peppers, broth, and celery.
- Enjoy with rice.

Amount per serving (12 total)

Timing Information:

Preparation	20 m
Cooking	8 h
Total Time	8 h 20 m

Nutritional Information:

Calories	235 kcal
Fat	13.6 g
Carbohydrates	6.1g
Protein	20.2 g
Cholesterol	99 mg
Sodium	688 mg

* Percent Daily Values are based on a 2,000 calorie diet.

Gumbo II

Ingredients

- 1 tbsp olive oil
- 1 C. skinless, boneless chicken breast halves - chopped
- 1/2 lb pork sausage links, thinly sliced
- 1 C. olive oil
- 1 C. all-purpose flour
- 2 tbsps minced garlic
- 3 quarts chicken broth
- 1 (12 fluid oz.) can or bottle beer
- 6 stalks celery, diced
- 4 roma (plum) tomatoes, diced
- 1 sweet onion, sliced
- 1 (10 oz.) can diced tomatoes with green chili peppers, with liquid
- 2 tbsps chopped fresh red chili peppers
- 1 bunch fresh parsley, chopped
- 1/4 C. Cajun seasoning
- 1 lb shrimp, peeled and deveined

Directions

- Stir fry your chicken in hot oil until fully done. Then add in your sausage and continue to stir fry until it is done as well.
- Place the contents in a bowl.
- In the same pan or a new one make a roux with flour and olive oil.
- Once it is brown add your garlic and stir fry the mix for 2 mins.
- Combine the following with your roux while stirring: beer, and broth.
- Get the roux simmering and then add: Cajun seasoning, celery, parsley, tomatoes, red chili peppers, sweet onions, diced tomatoes.
- Let your roux lightly boil with a covering for 45 mins with low heat.
- Stir the roux every 5 to 7 mins.
- Then combine in your sausage and chicken and simmer for 25 more mins.

- Enjoy.

Amount per serving (10 total)

Timing Information:

Preparation	1 h
Cooking	1 h
Total Time	2 h

Nutritional Information:

Calories	419 kcal
Fat	28.7 g
Carbohydrates	17.3g
Protein	20.5 g
Cholesterol	99 mg
Sodium	900 mg

* Percent Daily Values are based on a 2,000 calorie diet.

Jambalaya II

Ingredients

- 2 tbsps peanut oil, divided
- 1 tbsp Cajun seasoning
- 10 oz. andouille sausage, sliced into rounds
- 1 lb boneless skinless chicken breasts, cut into 1 inch pieces
- 1 onion, diced
- 1 small green bell pepper, diced
- 2 stalks celery, diced
- 3 cloves garlic, minced
- 1 (16 oz.) can crushed Italian tomatoes
- 1/2 tsp red pepper flakes
- 1/2 tsp ground black pepper
- 1 tsp salt
- 1/2 tsp hot pepper sauce
- 2 tsps Worcestershire sauce
- 1 tsp file powder
- 1 1/4 C. uncooked white rice
- 2 1/2 C. chicken broth

Directions

- Get a bowl, mix: chicken and sausage with Cajun seasoning.
- Then fry your seasoned meats in 2 tbsps of peanut oil in a Dutch oven until fully browned.
- Now put the meats in a 2nd bowl.
- Add to the same pot: garlic, onions, celery, and bell peppers.
- Stir the contents fry until everything is soft then add: hot sauce, file powder, red pepper, salt, Worcestershire, black pepper, and crushed tomatoes.
- Cook the mix for 5 mins then add your meats and cook everything for 13 more mins.
- Add the broth and the rice.
- Get everything boiling, set the heat to low, and let the contents simmer for 30 mins until all the liquid has evaporated.
- Enjoy.

Amount per serving (6 total)

Timing Information:

Preparation	20 m
Cooking	45 m
Total Time	1 h 5 m

Nutritional Information:

Calories	465 kcal
Fat	19.8 g
Carbohydrates	42.4g
Protein	28.1 g
Cholesterol	73 mg
Sodium	1633 mg

* Percent Daily Values are based on a 2,000 calorie diet.

Jambalaya III

Ingredients

- 8 skinless, boneless chicken breast halves - diced
- 6 C. chicken broth
- 3 C. long grain white rice
- 1 lb smoked sausage, sliced
- 1/4 C. vegetable oil
- 1 green bell pepper, seeded and chopped
- 1 small onion, finely chopped
- 4 carrots, thinly sliced
- 2 stalks celery, thinly sliced
- 1 (8 oz.) can mushroom pieces, drained
- 1/4 tsp cayenne pepper, or to taste
- salt and pepper to taste

Directions

- Stir fry your onions until tender, in oil, in a big pot.

- Then combine in your chicken and stir fry it until the chicken is browned evenly.
- Combine in the following with your chicken and onions: sausage, carrots, bell pepper, mushrooms, and celery.
- Cook this mix for 2 mins while stirring.
- Now add your broth and get it boiling.
- Once everything is boiling pour in your pepper, cayenne, salt, and rice.
- Place a lid on the pot, set the heat to a low level, and let the rice simmer for 22 mins.
- At this point all the liquid should have evaporated (if not continue simmering).
- Enjoy.

Amount per serving (12 total)

Timing Information:

Preparation	15 m
Cooking	25 m
Total Time	40 m

Nutritional Information:

Calories	463 kcal
Fat	18.9 g
Carbohydrates	42.2g
Protein	28.8 g
Cholesterol	71 mg
Sodium	711 mg

* Percent Daily Values are based on a 2,000 calorie diet.

Creole Style Chicken Breasts

Ingredients

- 1/4 lb bacon
- 4 skinless, boneless chicken breast halves - cut into strips
- 1 tsp Cajun seasoning
- 1 tbsp light olive oil
- 1 head romaine lettuce- rinsed, dried and chopped
- 1/2 C. Caesar salad dressing
- 1/3 C. grated Parmesan cheese

Directions

- Fry your bacon. Then break it into pieces and place it in a separate bowl.
- Now add your olive oil, seasonings, and chicken to the same pan.
- Fry the chicken until fully done and brown all over.

- Shut off the heat.
- Once the chicken has a cooled a bit slice it.
- Get a big bowl, combine: bacon, lettuce, parmesan, and salad dressing.
- Stir the salad with two large forks to coat the lettuce evenly with dressing then place the salad on serving dishes.
- On each dish add some chicken pieces.
- Enjoy.

Amount per serving (4 total)

Timing Information:

Preparation	15 m
Cooking	35 m
Total Time	50 m

Nutritional Information:

Calories	376 kcal
Fat	24.7 g
Carbohydrates	4.4g
Protein	32.6 g
Cholesterol	95 mg
Sodium	815 mg

* Percent Daily Values are based on a 2,000 calorie diet.

Bourbon Chicken

Ingredients

- 4 skinless, boneless chicken breast halves
- 1 tsp ground ginger
- 4 oz. soy sauce
- 2 tbsps dried minced onion
- 1/2 C. packed brown sugar
- 3/8 C. bourbon
- 1/2 tsp garlic powder

Directions

- Get a bowl, combine: garlic powder, ginger, bourbon, soy sauce, sugar, and onions flakes.
- Layer a casserole dish with the chicken.
- Then coat the chicken with your wet mix.
- Let the casserole sit in the fridge for at least 8 hours or throughout

the night covered with plastic wrap or a lid.
- Now set your oven to 325 degrees before doing anything else.
- Cook the chicken in the oven for 1.5 hours and baste it every 10 to 12 mins.
- Enjoy with rice.

Amount per serving (4 total)

Timing Information:

Preparation	10 m
Cooking	10 h
Total Time	10 h 10 m

Nutritional Information:

Calories	313 kcal
Fat	1.5 g
Carbohydrates	31.2g
Protein	29.3 g
Cholesterol	68 mg
Sodium	1664 mg

* Percent Daily Values are based on a 2,000 calorie diet.

Cajun Gumbo IV

Ingredients

- 1 C. vegetable oil
- 1 C. all-purpose flour
- 1 large onion, chopped
- 1 large green bell pepper, chopped
- 2 celery stalks, chopped
- 1 lb andouille or smoked sausage, sliced 1/4 inch thick
- 4 cloves garlic, minced
- salt and pepper to taste
- Creole seasoning to taste
- 6 C. chicken broth
- 1 bay leaf
- 1 rotisserie chicken, boned and shredded

Directions

- For 12 mins stir fry flour and oil to make a brown roux.

- But make sure your roux does not have any black dots in it.
- If so, try again.
- Now add the: sausage, onions, celery, and bell peppers.
- Cook this mix for 7 mins.
- Add in your garlic and let the contents cook for 6 more mins.
- Add: creole seasoning, pepper, broth, salt, and bay leaf.
- Get this all boiling and then set the heat to low and let the mix lightly cook for 1 hour.
- Finally add in your chicken and cook the contents for 1 more hour.
- Stir the mix every 10 mins.
- Enjoy.

Amount per serving (10 total)

Timing Information:

Preparation	45 m
Cooking	2 h 30 m
Total Time	3 h 15 m

Nutritional Information:

Calories	478 kcal
Fat	39.4 g
Carbohydrates	14.3g
Protein	16 g
Cholesterol	56 mg
Sodium	1045 mg

* Percent Daily Values are based on a 2,000 calorie diet.

Northeast Louisiana Style Cajun Wings with Sweet and Spicy Sauce

Ingredients

- 6 lbs chicken wings, separated at joints, tips discarded
- 1 1/2 C. Louisiana-style hot sauce
- 3/4 C. butter
- 1 C. honey
- 1 pinch garlic salt
- 1 pinch ground black pepper
- 1 tsp cayenne pepper, or to taste
- 1 tsp red pepper flakes

Directions

- You will need a grill for this recipe. So heat yours up after oiling the grate.
- Cook the chicken on the grill for 10 mins per side until fully done.

- Then place the chicken in a saucepan.
- In a 2nd saucepan boil the following for 12 mins: cayenne, hot sauce, black pepper, butter, garlic salt, and honey.
- Cover your wings in this wet sauce and finally sprinkle on the pepper flakes.
- Enjoy.

NOTE: Instead of using a grill, which is preferred you can fry then, bake these wings for a good taste as well. Fry the chicken first, then coat it with the sauce by tossing the wings in a bowl. Then bake them for a bit in the oven until crispy.

Amount per serving (12 total)

Timing Information:

Preparation	15 m
Cooking	30 m
Total Time	45 m

Nutritional Information:

Calories	356 kcal
Fat	22.7 g
Carbohydrates	23.9 g
Protein	15.6 g
Cholesterol	78 mg
Sodium	896 mg

* Percent Daily Values are based on a 2,000 calorie diet.

Bourbon Chicken II

Ingredients

- 4 tbsps olive oil
- 3 lbs skinless, boneless chicken breast halves - cut into 1 inch pieces
- 1 C. water
- 1 C. packed light brown sugar
- 3/4 C. apple-grape-cherry juice
- 2/3 C. soy sauce
- 1/4 C. ketchup
- 1/4 C. peach-flavored bourbon liqueur (such as Southern Comfort (R))
- 2 tbsps apple cider vinegar
- 2 cloves garlic, minced
- 1 tbsp dried minced onion
- 3/4 tsp crushed red pepper flakes, or to taste
- 1/2 tsp ground ginger
- 1/4 C. apple-grape-cherry juice
- 2 tbsps cornstarch

Directions

- Fry your chicken in a Dutch oven for 10 mins constantly stirring. Then place the chicken aside.
- Now add to the pot: ginger, water, red pepper, brown sugar, dried onion, 3/4 C. of fruit cocktail juice, garlic, soy sauce, vinegar, ketchup, and bourbon.
- Get this mix boiling and then add the chicken back in.
- Once everything is boiling again set the heat to low and simmer the mix until everything is thick for 20 mins.
- Take out the chicken again and place it aside with slotted spoon.
- Combine 1/4 C. fruit cocktail juice and cornstarch and then mix it with the sauce.
- Get the sauce boiling again for about 2 mins.
- Then add the chicken back to the mix and heat it through.
- Enjoy with rice.

Amount per serving (8 total)

Timing Information:

Preparation	15 m
Cooking	45 m
Total Time	1 h

Nutritional Information:

Calories	417 kcal
Fat	10.9 g
Carbohydrates	36.7g
Protein	37.1 g
Cholesterol	97 mg
Sodium	1382 mg

* Percent Daily Values are based on a 2,000 calorie diet.

Thanks for Reading! Now Let's Try some Sushi and Dump Dinners....

Send the Book!

To grab this **box set** simply follow the link mentioned above, or tap the book cover.

This will take you to a page where you can simply enter your email address and a PDF version of the **box set** will be emailed to you.

I hope you are ready for some serious cooking!

[Send the Book!](#)

You will also receive updates about all my new books when they are free.

Also don't forget to like and subscribe on the social networks. I love meeting my readers. Links to all my profiles are below so please click and connect :)

[Facebook](#)

[Twitter](#)

Come On...
Let's Be Friends :)

I adore my readers and love connecting with them socially. Please follow the links below so we can connect on Facebook, Twitter, and Google+.

Facebook

Twitter

I also have a blog that I regularly update for my readers so check it out below.

My Blog

Can I Ask A Favour?

If you found this book interesting, or have otherwise found any benefit in it. Then may I ask that you post a review of it on Amazon? Nothing excites me more than new reviews, especially reviews which suggest new topics for writing. I do read all reviews and I always factor feedback into my newer works.

So if you are willing to take ten minutes to write what you sincerely thought about this book then please visit our Amazon page and post your opinions.

Again thank you!

INTERESTED IN OTHER EASY COOKBOOKS?

Everything is easy! Check out my Amazon Author page for more great cookbooks:

For a complete listing of all my books please see my author page.

Printed in Great Britain
by Amazon